A Reason to Read

Linking Literacy and the Arts

Eileen Landay
Kurt Wootton

HARVARD EDUCATION PRESS
CAMBRIDGE, MASSACHUSETTS

Library of Congress Control Number 2012937485

Paperback ISBN 978-1-61250-460-5
Library Edition ISBN 978-1-61250-461-2

Published by Harvard Education Press,
an imprint of the Harvard Education Publishing Group

Harvard Education Press
8 Story Street
Cambridge, MA 02138

Cover Design and Photo: Sarah Henderson

The typefaces used in this book are Minion, ITC Novarese, and Helvetica Neue.

A Reason
to Read

We dedicate this book to
the memory of Ted Sizer,
who brought us together and
taught us to keep the focus
where it belongs—
on the essential relationship
between teachers and students.

Contents

Foreword

. . . the play's the thing
wherein I'll catch the conscience of the King.

—HAMLET, *II, ii*

WE OFTEN THINK of the power of play—or, indeed, of any performance—in terms of Hamlet's pronouncement. However, the context (and intent) of Hamlet's assignment of power as interpretive performance rarely enters into the thinking of those who may view the quotation merely as praise of what theater can do to force the audience into introspection. Hamlet refers here not simply to *a* play as *a* performance. He encompasses all that *play* means as human beings perform their roles throughout life: the imaginative entry into explorations of identity, chance, fate, celebration, and both social and solitary contemplation of "what if?" or "what about . . . ?"

A Reason to Read: Linking Literacy and the Arts offers readers the "Performance Cycle," a programmatic approach that leads to learning and literacy boosts. This book insists that readers come to grips with all the power that *play*—in its full range of meanings—has on what humans learn and how they come to think of themselves and others. Landay and Wootton brilliantly show how learning to read, write, interpret, and take roles in numerous genres leads to action, reflection, and collaboration. The young learners within this volume take part in a range of modes of learning, as well as meta-analysis of what happens when learners assume roles beyond themselves. Individuals write, sketch, deliberate, enact, and become dramaturgs and critics. Landay and Wootton reveal the work young people accomplish when they become immersed in communal affiliation as they develop, produce, and assess their joint performances. In doing so, young learners simulate not only their personal experiences, but also those of others they have known in their own lives and become acquainted with through their examination of literature, history, and popular culture. Young learners occupy a particular place, feeling, and process of interacting by mirroring the behaviors of their peers and other actors in everyday performance spaces, as well as in the multitude of digital entertainment platforms they engage with on a daily basis. However, as cognitive neuroscientists have pointed out, humans, unlike other higher-order primates, inevitably extend beyond simply mirroring what they see others do. Given a chance, they vary, tweak, and create anew. They interpret, so that their bodies, from head to toe, become instruments to convey meaning that they—as unique individuals—feel and know.

When they act like someone else, the learners in this book operate in a "liminal zone" between reality and an imagined world. They imagine by first writing and then by enacting the experiences and emotions portrayed in the texts they write and read. As they do so, they step into roles they have never played and may never play in their own real-world lives. Neuroscientists have shown the cognitive performance boost that comes when individuals risk taking on and interpreting roles that challenge them to be someone other than what they have believed themselves to be. As young learners look toward their roles, they use a variety of art forms to create scenes that become part of the expected process of fortifying the imagination—not only about the genres they read, but also about authors, historical and current figures in the public realm, and their own lives. Through all these figures, learners within the Performance Cycle (which this book centers on) examine intentions, points of view, and causes and effects. Young people engaged in all that the play world of the Performance Cycle offers have "reason to read" (and write). Taking on the mantle of others, whose emotions, heritage, and actions are laid out in various media (including written texts), offers young learners extensive practice in cognitive operations generally untouched within the passive student role associated with formal instructional settings.

The play of cognitive, emotional, and embodied performance is distributed. The work of this play belongs not just to the individual learner and player, but also to peers, written texts, and present and past interpreters (such as actors, reviewers, and critics; teachers and other students; and the contemporary audience for learners' productions and performances). There is always leeway for individual agency and interpretive slant or stance. Deliberative conversations circulate around the "rightness" of specific ways of putting oneself into a particular role. Judgments surround not only interpretations of particular parts, but also the nature of specific lines, scenes, and outcomes of portions of a novel or piece of history.

Inevitably, every enactment encircles young learners in the matter of moral responsibility. Individual learners playing roles can do so only by becoming socially aware of others within the play. Learners pulled into the Performance Cycle have to feel, see, and think through characters, situations, and contexts as they explore written texts across genres.

An additional double-edged cognitive benefit of enacting roles results from the intensity of the social awareness that comes from being in the midst of peers playing roles beyond the here and now. Individuals must be simultaneously self-reliant *and* responsive to the needs and moods of others. The empathetic immersion that comes from being a member of a performance group enables young people to develop a sense of what others need and to respond with actions and stances that portray accountability. Forms of play within any performance create situations in which emotive engagement by the players leads to interaction with various types of humanity living in circumstances that the players will likely never know.

The word *engrossment* rarely enters contemporary conversations about learning. However, this state of rapt engagement has long been the ideal result of aesthetic representations in theater, music, and visual art productions. For centuries, engrossment has stimulated contemplation and reflection, as viewers and listeners ask the ultimate question of any artistic representation: "What does this say/mean to me?" Forms of art, perhaps theater especially, always challenge the dominance of individual desire and self-satisfaction. As Landay and Wootton lay out not only the theory behind their Performance Cycle, but also the follow-through by teachers and young learners immersed in the cycle, they illustrate again and again where engrossment takes those who enter the play of the dramatic world.

Educators across fields will resonate with the literacy gains—through skills, accelerated appreciation, cumulative knowledge, and habituated practices of literacy—that the Performance Cycle opens for learners. Yet readers of the book should recognize that what is given here amounts to much more. Dramatics, or the performance of what is known and felt, enables players not only to interpret and act but also to envision. By preparing for the roles they play, individuals practice and thereby habituate the steps necessary to look into where and how they must plan for the future. The habits that surround planning do not come easily for young people in modern life, since they talk and think about the present. Yet without extensive practice in planning step-by-step, practicing to perform in a certain way, and responding through improvisation and adaption to others, the young have no framework for envisioning their own futures. The critical role of envisionment—developing strong and deep images of a desired future and constructing the process by which one can get there—may well be the most important gift of the Performance Cycle.

For young people living in modern economies, what generally matters most in learning is motivated, practiced, perfected, adapted, or abandoned within their own frameworks of what is meaningful to them. Being locked in the present self means that they limit much of their language to talking about what's happening now. They avoid expressing conditional and comparative thinking that asks "what if?" or "what about . . . ?" History, memory, and the complexities of the world beyond them do not often penetrate their reasoning or enlist their emotions or intellects.

Yet few young learners can resist the thrill of the ups and downs of the Performance Cycle or the embrace of the learning community it generates. Here in the play—the give and take, action and reflection of performance—the young ready themselves for the participation culture that marks the future they face. The world is shifting rapidly away from the authoritative model of information that is filtered by experts and given to novices. Already, learning has moved toward a distributed model in which creativity, design, assessment, and transmission of bits of information prevail.

Play and the arts have always affirmed that our very humanity gives us a network of cognitive and emotive operations. Taken together, our ideas, imagination, values, morals, desires, and beliefs enable us to take part in performance cycles throughout life. The younger we are when we begin learning to do so, the better. Learning through playing "as if" or "what about" may well be the preparation that matters most in the long run, because new and different roles within our individual performance cycles mark the passage of years and the alterations and loss of those relationships we hold dearest. Practice of the Performance Cycle model and reflection on all that it means show that it prepares us for the consequences and meanings of the range of performances our lives offers us.

But enough about all that the world of performance brings to the literary, dramatic, and, above all, creative and interpretive platforms of the arts. Landay and Wootton have with clear and loving detail opened for us the meanings that teachers and learners together have explored, discovered, and represented in the Performance Cycle. My hope is that you will follow my enthusiasm and turn the page. Bring on the play!

Shirley Brice Heath
STANFORD UNIVERSITY

Introduction

We who are teachers would have to accommodate ourselves to lives as clerks or functionaries if we did not have in mind a quest for a better state of things for those we teach and for the world we all share. It is simply not enough for us to reproduce the way things are.

—Maxine Greene

IMAGINE FOR A MOMENT that it's the first day of school and you are a high school junior named Anthony.[1] *As fifth period begins, you're headed toward room 209A. It's a long walk down a fluorescent-lit corridor, through streaming crowds of strangers and, once in a while, past someone you know. A short pause, a quick high five, and on you go, weaving through the current of talk, music, moving bodies, slamming locker doors. Inside the classroom, silence. Thirty chairs in rows. Students waiting for class to begin. A teacher up front waiting for the bell to ring. Welcome to English class.*

It's all so familiar. Yet even on this first day of school, you don't feel any real connection with what goes on in this room. You know you're supposed to graduate. Go to college. Get a good job. You've heard it all a million times. Ever since third grade, teachers have told you that what they are teaching will make a huge difference in your life. It's never worked out that way. Last year you squeaked by with Ds and one C.

You take a seat and look around. The teacher looks familiar. You've passed her in the hall, been in classes with a few of these kids before, but you don't

1

really know any of them. Your thoughts wander. Time passes. You realize the teacher has been talking but you haven't really been listening. Now she's passing out heavy thick books. In your mind, the year stretches ahead endlessly. You feel you really don't belong here, in this room, with these people. You wish you were some place—anyplace—else. Suddenly, you are very tired. You feel yourself slumping in your seat. You want to put your head down to go to sleep.

We begin this book by asking you to imagine *being* Anthony, to see what he sees, to think his thoughts, to do your best to live—if only for a few moments—inside his mind and his body. Our purpose is not only to offer a portrait of a person in a challenging situation but also to introduce a pedagogy we have been developing during the past dozen years to address the challenges Anthony, his teacher, and the students in his class are likely to face, an approach we describe in detail in this book.

Were we to explore Anthony's situation in depth, we would ask you to enter his world as fully as possible by raising a series of questions about who he is, what he knows and cares about, and the specifics of his daily life in school. We would ask you to bring Anthony's story to life by exploring these questions through one or more media—improvisation, visual arts, music, dance—and then engage in a series of activities that combines and integrates literacy and the arts. We would ask you to read more about Anthony as well as other students who are very different from him. Working together, we would talk, think, write, then create a *performance of understanding* that responds to the initial questions we raised as we explored his story.[2] We might begin with a question like, "How can we create a learning environment that students find relevant, challenging, and worthy of their attention and effort?"

Those of us who teach have known many, many Anthonys. Our challenge, and indeed our responsibility, lies in doing our best to help Anthony and every other student we encounter to connect, absorb, and make use of the course content and processes to grow and develop as thinking, fully functioning human beings who contribute in positive ways to the world. Some students come to school believing academic content is relevant to their lives, understanding the small steps that will lead to academic success, and being willing and able to take those steps. Others give these beliefs lip service but not the necessary effort. Yet others have never been convinced that school matters either to their present or future lives. By the time they reach secondary school, many have a history of failure that has become both a pattern and an expectation that limits and diminishes their sense of who they are and what they can become. This perspective is exactly the opposite of what we educators want schooling to accomplish.

For the past dozen years, a group of teachers and artists based in the Education Department at Brown University have worked to create learning environments that bring academic content to life. The major focus of the enterprise we named the ArtsLiteracy Project has been to enrich literacy pedagogy through the arts. Our goal has been to design environments that help students develop receptivity, focus, effort, and the ability to think, learn, create, and reflect. In doing this work, we ask what it means to be a literate person and how we can best create rich, memorable learning opportunities for students.

WHAT IS LITERACY AND WHY ACQUIRE IT?

Derived from the Latin *litteratus*, in its most literal meaning, *literacy* refers to an acquaintance with letters. In this sense, it has been defined as "the ability to read and write a simple message."[3] In the current-day context, however, educators recognize that literacy goes far beyond merely understanding and communicating simple messages with print texts. We understand that literacy and the pedagogy of literacy have become more complex and multifaceted and, simultaneously, more crucially tied to students' social futures.[4]

Some years ago, a group of international literacy educators, the New London Group, convened to explore the way that literacy is developing and changing. The group coined the term *multiliteracies*. The prefix *multi-* points in two directions: first, to the multiplicity of channels for communication and comprehension that includes, but extends far beyond, print;

and, second, to the cultural and linguistic diversity most people encounter in this increasingly global society. In the first sense, the term refers to the plurality of text types and forms that circulate and connect, the "increasing multiplicity and integration of significant modes of meaning-making, where the textual is also related to the visual, the audio, the spatial, the behavioral, and so on."[5] In the second sense, multiliteracies refers to the multiple languages and communication patterns each of us is likely to encounter, the broadening range of specialist registers and situational variations that more and more frequently cross cultural, national, and community boundaries.

Every day in classrooms, teachers encounter the full range of multiliteracies. We meet some students who are proficient readers and writers, skilled at academic literacy; others who are talented visual artists or musicians who struggle to master high school–level print texts; those who speak three or four languages with ease but resist putting pen to paper; and still others expert at negotiating the rich and complex world of the Internet. As options and variations increase, so too does the evidence that students' experiences in school—and with literacy pedagogy in particular—contribute in major ways to their life chances. Their school achievements are closely tied to their prospects in the years beyond and to the creation of their social futures. What happens to Anthony in the next few minutes—and in the days beyond—really matters.

By the time students reach high school, they have developed an *identity kit* of personal goals and interests closely tied to the kinds of literacies they practice.[6] They have a long history of school success and failure, often based on their facility in mastering traditional literacy forms and processes. Their histories affect how they see themselves as well as how others see them and contribute in major ways to their educational outcomes and life opportunities.

MULTILITERACIES AND POSITIVE SOCIAL FUTURES

How might educators design and establish classrooms in which a student's academic history is not a predictor of her social destiny? How might we create academic environments that inspire rather than limit, that incorporate the full range of multiliteracies, and that support students in developing a range of skills, knowledge, and dispositions they can use to participate fully and productively in public, community, and economic life? These are formidable and critical questions. To address them requires a vision for what such environments can accomplish and a design for bringing these environments to life, what Maxine Greene describes as a "quest for a better state of things."[7]

As educators, we assume responsibility for developing that vision and design. As mentors, our ideas need to be transparent and explicit enough that our students can both adopt and adapt the vision and modify the design for their own purposes. The kinds of sharing we have in mind involve: (1) giving students access to materials and ideas that open new educational and social possibilities and help them to establish their own personal vision; and (2) encouraging them to connect actively with content, "to develop the capacity to speak up, to negotiate and to engage critically with the conditions of their working lives."[8] As the New London Group points out, the combination of access and critical engagement motivates students to develop and refine the tools they require to design their social futures.

At the ArtsLiteracy Project we began to explore ways to link literacy and the arts in order to bring to the learning environment the full range of multiliteracies. We imagined classrooms in which students learn to be active and skilled readers, writers, speakers, listeners, and creators, all in the service of exploring and addressing significant issues in their lives and the lives of others. We imagined methods of inquiry in which students connect their interests, personal stories, and questions to the rich storehouse of existing literary and artistic texts. We believe students can use this process to design and construct positive social futures.

In the pages that follow, we describe this approach, agreeing with educational historian Diane Ravitch that no "silver bullet . . . magic feather . . . or panacea will miraculously improve student achievement."[9] Instead, we offer our experience as a modest example of an approach that brings to life and makes transparent our vision of what education can be. At its best, this approach welcomes students into the world of learning, promotes civility and mutual respect among participants, and offers a balance between rich academic content and the tools for working with that content.

In articulating this vision, we draw on the work of many who have preceded us—philosophers, educators, researchers, and theorists. Three who have influenced our work are educator Paulo Freire, philosopher Maxine Greene, and linguistic anthropologist and researcher Shirley Brice Heath. Freire was a passionate believer in the power and value of literacy to make sense of a difficult and confusing world and, ultimately, to create positive social change. His education project, developed in Brazil and implemented worldwide, is famously based on three elements: establishing an environment of mutual respect in which serious dialogue among equals can take place, developing participants' critical consciousness, and putting literacy learning to work in the service of equity and social justice. In Freire's view, the purpose of developing literacy must not be to replicate existing knowledge but, rather, to use inquiry to assist reason: "Apart from inquiry . . . individuals cannot be truly human. Knowledge emerges only through invention and re-invention, through the restless, impatient, continuing, hopeful inquiry human beings pursue in the world, with the world, and with each other."[10] Freire described environments in which people saw literacy learning as tied to their own self-interest as "pockets of hope": "The people wanted and needed to read and to write, precisely in order to have more of a possibility to be themselves . . . Reading and writing was an important instrument and also a sign of respect for them, self-respect."[11]

Like Freire, Maxine Greene's project is aimed at creating positive social change, or "looking at things as if they could be otherwise." Greene views the arts as a powerful tool for releasing the imagination, opening new perspectives, and identifying alternatives: "To tap into imagination is to become able to break with what is supposedly fixed and finished . . . and to carve out new orders in experience . . . what might be, what should be and what is not yet." She identifies writers, painters, sculptors, filmmakers, choreographers, and composers as creating "as if" worlds in which work in the arts leads to appreciating cultural diversity, making community, and becoming wide-awake to the world.

> What I am describing here is a mode of . . . thinking that refuses mere compliance, that looks down roads not yet taken to the shapes of a more fulfilling social order, to more vibrant ways of being in the world. That kind of reshaping imagination may be released through many sorts of dialogue: dialogue among the young who come from different cultures and different modes of life, dialogue among people who have come together to solve problems that seem worth solving to all of them, dialogue among people undertaking shared tasks, protesting injustices, avoiding or overcoming dependencies or illnesses. When such dialogue is activated in classrooms even the young are stirred to reach out on their own initiatives. Apathy and indifference are likely to give way as images of what might be arise.[12]

Recently, researchers have begun to use large data sets and analytical tools such as the fMRI to study the links between the arts and cognition. Some of this work explores the effects of what researchers variously call *embodied learning, kinesthetic learning,* or *mimesis,* situations in which people use their bodies to represent specific content. Others study the learner's attentional capacity, short- and long-term memory, and the effects of presenting material using a variety of symbol systems. Still others seek to identify ways that learning in the arts may transfer to learning in other content areas. Behind all of these approaches is the premise that multisensory learning—theatrical improvisation, visual art, writing, dancing, and singing in combination with the study of a challenging literary text—provides a developmentally appropriate means of engaging students, especially adolescents, with new ideas, with their own creativity, and with one another.

We began to see possibilities for moving from theory to practice in Shirley Brice Heath and Milbury W. McLaughlin's research on arts-based youth organizations. In an extensive, decade-long survey of 124 youth organizations in the United States, Heath, McLaughlin, and a team of researchers examined the multiple roles youth play in these organizations.

They took a particularly close look at language and found that "the influences of participation in the arts on language shows up in the dramatic increase in syntactic complexity, hypothetical reasoning, and questioning approaches taken up by young people within four-to-six weeks of their entry into the arts organization."[13] Furthermore, "students in theatre-based organizations of our research had in each practice session approximately six times as many opportunities to speak more than one sentence as they might have in their English and Social Studies classrooms." Students in community arts organizations practice "thinking and talking as adults." They have a side-by-side relationship with the mentoring adults in the organizations. Heath explains that "the highly frequent oral exchanges between youth and older peers and adults around problem posing and hypothetical reasons lead these youth in arts organizations to consider multiple ways of doing and being in their artistic work and beyond."

With these findings in mind, we began to ask why students don't participate at the same level during school hours as they do in community-based arts organizations. Might we envision a process where students and teachers engage collaboratively in imagining creative possibilities and developing authentic artistic products? Can the kind of hypothetical thinking and discussion that exists in arts-based youth organizations be part of the daily life of schools?

TRANSLATING VISION INTO PRACTICE: THE ARTSLITERACY PROJECT

The goal of the ArtsLiteracy Project is to create powerful learning experiences that have the capacity to transform participants' understanding and actions. Given that literacy achievement often determines student success in school, we wanted multiliteracies (including print texts and a range of other art forms) to anchor the work and to create communities of practice that use arts and literacy activities to promote collaboration, creativity, and literate behaviors.[14] We wanted participants to address significant questions, to explore them through carefully studying core texts, to use those texts and their own multiliteracies to explore, create, and perform responses to their questions. Finally, we wanted everyone involved to reflect on both the content and process of their learning.

Since its founding, the ArtsLiteracy Project has involved students of all ages, from elementary school to graduate school, and a wide-ranging group of teachers and artists. The center of the organization was a summer lab school on the campus at Brown University, the Brown Summer High School. Modeled on the design of Brown's Teacher Education Program, the lab school provided a space for artists and teachers to teach collaboratively in a supportive environment. High school–age students attended for little or no cost. On this site, we developed the principles and practices that became the ArtsLiteracy Project's framework and methods. During the school year, ArtsLiteracy supported literacy learning in public and independent school classrooms in several cities in the United States and, over the course of time, began working beyond the United States, particularly in Brazil, Mexico, and the Dominican Republic. Artists, teachers, and students explored key texts—including Shakespeare, Sandra Cisneros, Ovid, Whitman, Rudolfo Anaya, Octavio Paz—and created performances of their responses to the text for their peers in schools and for the community. Over ten years, we documented, discussed, and revised our work.

As we reviewed our strongest efforts, we noticed a common set of processes and practices emerging across classrooms. After much discussion, we formalized these processes into a pedagogical framework that we called the Performance Cycle.[15] We shared this framework with colleagues in curriculum development and professional development workshops. Teachers and artists used the Performance Cycle to design instruction in a range of settings and with students of every age, from preschool programs to university theater, language, and literature courses. They tell us they find it a logical and useful planning structure applicable in a range of settings and with many different types of content.

THE PERFORMANCE CYCLE

The Performance Cycle, while not prescriptive, offers teachers and learners a shared approach and a common vocabulary. Both clear and flexible, this relatively simple design allows room for adaptation and innovation. It places trust and responsibility in teachers and students and acknowledges the importance of context, variation in settings, funds of knowledge, and individual goals and purposes.[16]

The cycle begins with *Building Community* (see figure I.1). Introductory activities create a constructive environment where students come to know and respect one another so that learning can readily take place. In such classrooms, teachers and artists create spaces in which students feel they are known and appreciated. Students understand the purpose of the work and value their own roles in the creation and collaboration that takes place.[17]

FIGURE I.1
The Performance Cycle

Having begun to establish a community of learners, students are then invited to *Enter Text*. They are now introduced to essential questions, topics, and themes that establish connections between the academic content and their own lives. They begin to explore the language, characters, and plot of a core print text through multiple art forms, including visual art, dance, music, and theater. This generative environment encourages them to develop receptivity to learning about topics and trying out new skills. Students expand their learning horizons, the breadth of topics that they find interesting, relevant, and worthy of their attention.

Students next engage in a range of activities that focus on *Comprehending Text*. Activities focus on reading, writing, and communication skills. Based on the current version of Bloom's Taxonomy, which classifies levels of intellectual behavior, learning objectives include remembering, understanding, applying, analyzing, evaluating, and creating.[18] Students interact with text in ways that involve both intensive and extensive reading. In other words, they read both deeply and widely. For example, students read to themselves or with peers, hear the text read out loud, work with partners to discuss the text, and consult ancillary materials. Activities focus on plot, themes, vocabulary, language, style, and texture of the central texts. Students perform lines or scenes using performance techniques previously introduced. Repeated purposeful engagement with text helps to increase their focus, stamina, and ability to engage an extended text in order to follow the thread of a story or an argument.

In *Creating Text,* students respond to essential questions and themes with their own interpretations and personal responses. Student write in mediums that include playwriting, poetry, personal narrative, analytical essay, monologue, or short stories and work in a variety of other art forms, such as dance, original music, visual art, and video. These activities are designed to explore spaces around a text by, for example, examining possibilities of what might happen after a text ends, between scenes, in the minds of characters, or in the lives of similar characters in similar times and places. The students then create texts that they combine with portions of the core text to create the final performance.

In *Rehearsing and Revising Text,* students modify, improve, and practice their performance. Throughout revision, students give and receive feedback on their own and one another's work. This feedback from peers, teachers and artists allows for continuous assessment and improvement. Attention to revision provides a key element for furthering students' literacy skills. At this stage, participants address three main concerns: (1) the quality of students' understanding and comfort with the original text; (2) the quality of students' creative responses; and (3) students' comfort with giving a public performance.

Finally, students *Perform Text.* Through their performance, students demonstrate what they have learned by performing for one another, peers, teachers, family, and friends in a relatively high-stakes but supportive environment. The performance is an original work that combines selections from the original text with student work. Guest artists may contribute to making the performance a high-quality event.

At the center of the Performance Cycle is *Reflection,* the process of participants becoming mindful of their own learning and the overall learning environment. From five-minute activities to entire days of classroom work, reflection through debriefing lies at the heart of ArtsLiteracy work. The cycle includes continuous reflection to ensure that teachers, artists, and students consistently engage in thinking and talking about their work as a way to highlight successes and areas for improvement as well as to make visible what everyone in the community is learning. Whenever possible, experienced mentors help facilitate the reflection process.

The Performance Cycle provides the basic structure for this book. Each chapter covers one section of the cycle and contains examples of ArtsLiteracy work in school and afterschool programs serving elementary age through college students, in summer and academic-year programs, and in urban and rural settings in the United States, Brazil, and Mexico. You will meet many ArtsLiteracy teachers. You will read about the extraordinary work of numerous teachers, artists, and students.

It would be a huge disservice to you the reader to suggest that pairing literacy and the arts and using the Performance Cycle as a framework for curriculum design offers an easy and foolproof solution to the challenges you face every day. Though we illustrate each chapter and each step in the Performance Cycle with "success stories," it would be dishonest not to acknowledge that we have experienced difficult moments, setbacks, disappointments. Teaching is hard and exceedingly demanding work. It requires inspiration, planning, practice, and support. To that end, we offer the chapters that follow as examples of a useful and flexible set of classroom tools—yours to adapt and apply as your interest and circumstances warrant. We intend this approach as a corrective to the top-down, uniform, prescriptive approach that is coming to be standard practice in many school districts, one that fails to balance the needs of the individual with the needs of the institution or to take into account the importance of context.

We want to begin the ArtsLiteracy story by returning for a moment to our student Anthony. We presented his brief portrait to imagine how the world looks and feels through his eyes. Anthony is the test against which we measure our work and the perspective from which we define success. Will what we teachers do make sense to Anthony? What will draw him in? What will give him the confidence to try? To practice? To become an expert? What does Anthony think it takes to learn something well?

In her recent research, Kathleen Cushman gathered a group of 160 teenagers from nine U.S. cities to address questions of this sort. Written for an audience of teachers, the students in *Fires in the Mind* reflect on what inspires and helps them learn. They describe developing interest and the initial steps they take toward expertise, the kinds of support that keep them going through difficult times, and, specifically, how teachers can help throughout. In summarizing her research, Cushman writes,

> The classroom, kids agreed, should . . . introduce them to new interests and exciting exemplars from the world of ideas in action. They hoped for adult guides who knew their strengths and believed in their potential. Expertise in academic subjects . . . flowed from what kids already valued and from their opportunities to try new things. It thrived on their close relationships and

on practice sessions tailored just for them. Its rewards came from within and from the recognition and respect of others.[19]

Relationships and opportunities, far more than innate talent, first drew these young people into the activities that engaged them most. Someone important to them offered a chance to explore something together. Many of these activities were kinesthetic in nature. Learning a sport, planting a garden, playing an instrument, repairing a car, baking bread, making a video—the purpose for practicing each of these activities is clear, explicit, visible. Students point out that all of the elements of this type of learning can and should be transferred to the more abstract or decontextualized material they are expected to learn in school.

The ArtsLiteracy Project puts these principles into practice. In the pages that follow, we describe and offer examples. Chapter 1 presents an overview of the Performance Cycle, describing each of its elements and how it can be applied, and chapters 2–8 address specific components of the cycle. The "For the Classroom" sections at the end of each chapter describe key activities that demonstrate the concepts presented in that chapter. Many of these activities have been selected from the online ArtsLiteracy Handbook, a compendium of activities that artists and teachers created in the ArtsLiteracy lab school at Brown Summer High School. These activities have withstood the test of time. We consistently use them in our practice and find them to be successful with participants of every age, from preschoolers to adults.

When used to further the ideas, concepts, or themes presented in each chapter, these activities serve as catalysts for building the classroom community, exploring a work of literature, helping students create written and artistic responses to text, and shaping performances that demonstrate the richness of our students' work. The goal is to create memorable literacy experiences for students, to engage them and help them learn and grow.

1

The Performance Cycle

Integrated arts education is designed to promote transfer of learning between the arts and other subjects, between the arts and the capacities students need to become successful adults. It is designed to use the emotional, social, and sensory dimensions of the arts to engage students and leverage development and learning across the curriculum . . . We might call it the arts for learning's sake.

—Nick Rabkin

"RUSSELL, I'D LIKE you to come out now," said Kevin Gibbs, a teaching artist.[1] There was no answer from inside the curtain. On the first day of Kevin's visit to Bobby Marchand's class at Central Falls High School in Central Falls, Rhode Island, Kevin and Bobby began the class on the stage in the school's auditorium. As the students gathered in a circle ready to participate in a series of performance activities, Russell left the group and wrapped himself 'round and 'round in the velvet curtain. Students looked in his direction, but no one laughed. In Bobby's classroom, students and teachers had learned to be patient with one another.

The students were used to Russell's ongoing issues. Bobby described Russell as "unique. Very rarely talked. Silent guy. He was the brunt of some unbelievable bullying." When Russell first became a part of Bobby's class, the other students in the classroom made fun of him. In Bobby's words, "He was the victim of the worst kind of school teasing teenagers can inflict on each other. Then, one day, after a particularly cruel episode in the hallways, one of my students said, 'You know, Russell doesn't bother anybody. Russell, you're all right. So, first of all, we're not going to pick on you and second of all we'll be on the lookout for you.'" Bobby laughed, "And you know I had plenty of desperados in my class, lots of tough guys, so Russell wasn't picked on again!"[2]

Despite the change in students' attitudes, Russell often came to class angry and refused to participate. Sometimes he put his head on his desk and pretended to sleep. Russell's classmates ignored his inappropriate behavior or joked with him when he was in good spirits. But on this day he was overwhelmed by the prospect of performing. Today, Russell needed time and space, and he found it on the school stage, hiding wrapped in a curtain.

Kevin encouraged, "Russell, we're going to start class. Please join us." Kevin knew enough not to try to force Russell to participate by threatening him with a low grade or by sending him out of class. The students in Bobby's class had faced the ire of teachers their entire school careers, so much so that the school created this self-contained class just for them: seven students, a teacher, and a teacher's assistant. Bobby was given classroom supplies appropriate to an elementary school classroom. He was told to manage students' behavior, to develop their practical skills (counting money, balancing a checkbook, interviewing for a job), and to offer basic literacy instruction mainly in the form of a regular diet of worksheets and workbooks.

Bobby knew there must be a better way to reach his students by having high, rather than low, expectations. To add to his repertoire of skills, the previous summer Bobby had signed up to teach at the ArtsLiteracy's lab school at the Brown Summer High School. There he met and partnered with actor Kevin Gibbs. Using the Performance Cycle model, they and their students read Shakespeare's *Othello*, wrote their own stories related to the play's themes, and performed those stories in combination with portions of the play. During the following school year, Kevin and Bobby were once again teaching partners. For one or two days a week for eight weeks, Kevin visited Bobby's Central Falls classroom. Together they and the students began work on a unit called "Insiders and Outsiders."

Measured by standardized tests, these students were far from proficient. Bobby explained, "The reading level in my class was consistent year after year, student after student. It wasn't just one group of kids. They always scored at the absolute lowest level, so much so that when I'd tell my students there would be testing, inevitably one of my students would say, 'They just want to see how dumb we are.'"

Bobby and Kevin planned for the class to read and respond to S. E. Hinton's *The Outsiders,* write stories of their own experiences as both insiders and outsiders, and create a performance of their work for other students. The teacher and actor believed that the topic and the process would be intriguing enough to capture the students' interest, encourage real effort, and help them learn. But today, with one of the seven students refusing to participate, any sort of performance seemed unlikely.

In our experience, many students hide inside a curtain, though obviously more metaphorical than real. Howard Gardner notes that the primary abilities or intelligences valued by schools are the linguistic and logical-mathematical.[3] Students who do adequately well with math and reading and behave appropriately usually graduate. Bobby's students were barely making it. Placed in traditional classrooms, students like Bobby's often disrupt or ignore: they put their heads down on their desk; they crack jokes and clown; they arrive late to school; they are often absent; they attend less and less often, and, finally, many drop out.

Bobby and Kevin believed students could do more than learn simple math or the social norms of a job interview. They were certain the students had funds of knowledge to draw on and significant questions they wanted to explore. They believed that as part of a community of practice, students could read and discuss important ideas and challenging texts. They knew the students had stories to tell and could write extensive narratives with rich description and dialogue. They believed the students were capable of offering something new to their community by creating an original performance in which all of them would have major roles. They wanted their students to come out from behind their proverbial curtain to see that they had reasons to read, learn, stay in school, and contribute positively to the work of the group.

Bobby and Kevin's "Insiders and Outsiders" unit was one of many developed by teachers and artists who participated in the ArtsLiteracy Project. Working collaboratively over the course of ten years, teachers, high school and college students, artists, and university faculty created and taught together in summer and academic-year courses and workshops. They worked in a range of high school and college classrooms with all types of students. In these courses, teachers, artists, and students explored questions and topics that linked students' lived experiences with the content of challenging texts. They designed activities that integrated literacy and the visual and performing arts. Using the Performance Cycle model (see fig. I.1), they created and presented original performances that demonstrated their understanding of what they had learned. At several sites—including local middle schools and high schools, a summer enrichment program for high school students, and an academic year college class at Brown University—a group of us developed, documented, and shared our work.

We found that students were engaged by using the Performance Cycle model to link literacy and the arts. Establishing a bridge between students' lives and a topic or content provided the impetus for them to comprehend a core text and create an original work that would culminate in a performance of understanding. The performance might be brief and informal, coming at the end of a single class period, or extended and detailed, as was the *Insiders and Outsiders* performance Russell's class eventually created. Over time, we developed each of the elements of the cycle and applied it in a wide range of settings.

BUILDING COMMUNITY

In Literacy, Community, and the Arts, the course we developed and taught from 1998 to 2006 for Brown University undergraduates and graduate students, each student wrote a literacy autobiography. Virtually every one of their stories described a relationship with at least one person—parent, friend, teacher—who loved and mentored them and inspired them to become fluent readers and writers. Many described hearing family members read to them at an early age.[4] One student wrote, "Me at age five with my older brother and my twin all perched (as I remember it) on my father's belly while he lay in bed reading J. R. R. Tolkien's *Lord of the Rings* aloud. If only my father's voice could continue the story forever!"[5]

While their presence in an Ivy League university classroom testified to their academic achievements, the students who wrote these essays came from a rich mix of ethnic, social, and economic backgrounds. We were struck by how vividly they described the connection between these literacy events and their academic development. What would it take, we wondered, to create classrooms where all students could experience a similar level of support, where in addition to supporting one's intellectual development, the act of reading and writing would forge warm relationships among its members? Such a climate may exist in the very early grades in classrooms but appears to diminish and usually disappears as students grow. Anonymity in daily life in school—especially large, urban secondary schools—is hardly news to anyone who has spent much time in them. The potential for a classroom to be a community often goes unrealized.

Our experience in schools has demonstrated the value of community building in secondary school literacy work. When students feel they are in a supportive community—filled with what we refer to with the Portuguese word *alegria*—they are willing to focus, work hard, and take risks.[6] Community is built in students' and teachers' hearts, and there are no easy games or gimmicks for achieving it in the classroom. Nonetheless, we have learned the importance of creating an environment in the classroom that encourages students to share their work and make genuine efforts to learn and grow.

Learning takes place most effectively in situations where people feel a sense of belonging to a group whose purposes and activities matter to them and can help them grow in ways they find rewarding. Students benefit from knowing that they are important to the other members of the community.[7] A productive learning environment is created by establishing a *shared purpose, supportive relationships*, and a *regular repertoire of routines and activities* in the classroom. "Engagement in social practice is the fundamental process by which we learn and so become who we are."[8]

Building a community "does not necessarily refer to a sense of harmony but, rather, a shared set of social practices and goals."[9] When a group of learners sets out to explore, create, and perform their response to a theme or compelling question, the ultimate purpose of their learning is clear and meaningful. Supportive relationships include connections between adults and students as well as between students and between adults. Routines are the daily activities that build group identity. They focus participants' attention and energy; offer clear, specific ways for people to connect and interact; and establish a tone of active engagement, play, and pleasure combined with seriousness of purpose. They are designed to introduce community members to one another, to foster respect for the resources that each person brings, and to build a positive learning environment.

Bobby stands in the classroom doorway at the beginning of every class and shakes his students' hands as they enter the room. As teacher and coach of the school's championship soccer team, Bobby gives his students an infusion of encouragement and energy. His students joke and laugh with him. When visitors enter the classroom, Bobby makes sure the students are not anonymous by asking them to introduce themselves.

From the beginning of the school year, Bobby leads students in physical warm-ups and vocal activities. These include stretches and movement exercises. Calling out tongue twisters like "red leather, yellow leather" and "you know you need unique New York," students practice oral language skills and hear their voices speaking out in a classroom setting. Trust-building activities give community members opportunities to know one another, to respect the resources that each person brings to the classroom, and to build supportive relationships. Community-building activities provide a foundation for text-based work by ensuring a supportive learning environment. Students know from the outset their work has a purpose and that they are creating a performance that will tell their stories to the community at large. To accomplish this purpose, they engage in questioning, collaborative planning, improvisation, reading, writing, discussion, critique, and reflection. Bobby and Kevin know that after having worked through the Performance Cycle once, the class will begin a second round with a far greater sense of cohesion and solidarity.

Although Bobby has been working for some time to build a strong sense of community, on the morning when Kevin asked the students to step on the stage to form a circle, Russell immediately took hold of the stage's curtain and wrapped himself in its many layers. After encouraging Russell to come out, Kevin joined the other students and began to lead them in community-building activities. Russell remained behind the curtain. When we asked Bobby how he reacted to Russell hiding in the curtain, he said, "I tried to talk him out. The curtain was old and dusty. When that didn't work, I said, 'Russell, you don't have to participate but just stand there.'" Bobby didn't cajole Russell out of the curtain or threaten to send him to the office. He encouraged but didn't force him to give up the protection of the curtain. Instead, they engaged in conversations designed to draw him back into the "classroom." Together, Bobby and Kevin moved ahead to create the kind of interesting and supportive community they believed Russell would eventually want to join.

ENTERING TEXT

In *Acting, Learning, and Change,* a book that has substantially influenced the ArtsLiteracy Project, Jan Mandell and Jennifer Wolf describe the *receptive mind:*

> The receptive mind is a ready mind—ready to welcome the challenge that comes with taking in new knowledge. It is confident and willing and curi-

ous, without being overly judgmental. The receptive mind concentrates on a task for productive lengths of time, even through distractions. The receptive mind carries on conversations with itself: pondering, trying out, and critiquing. Rather than a mind that contains a certain type of intelligence, it is a mind that knows when to use the many different intelligences it contains.[10]

Activities in the Performance Cycle help students to develop receptivity and combat the kinds of learned helplessness often cultivated unintentionally in schools when students attend in the most minimal ways, do little to engage with the contents of curriculum, copy directly from text, and exert the least possible effort to engage with and comprehend material.[11]

Receptivity and interest set in motion with community-building activities are further developed by addressing questions, themes, and language designed to increase curiosity, encourage students to develop interest in the topic at hand, form connections between the topic and their own lives, and explore the language of texts in helpings small enough not to be daunting. When a unit of study is designed around questions adolescents can understand and wonder about, that unit establishes a clear purpose and issues an invitation to students to learn, grow, and contribute to a body of knowledge they can immediately understand is significant. Educators call these *essential questions*.[12] These questions "provoke deep thought, lively discussion, sustained inquiry, and new understanding as well as more questions."[13] They are quite distinct from the kinds of factual, short-answer, right-or-wrong-answer questions teachers are most commonly known to ask.

Some students are good at working with complex text; they are able to look at a novel, an essay, or a textbook to see its ideas or narrative played out like a movie in their heads. Others merely see words on a page.[14] Along this continuum, students' reading comprehension may be entirely unrelated to their own receptivity, curiosity, or interests. In the Entering Text phase of the Performance Cycle, students are introduced to questions and topics through the arts and by working with brief, evocative portions of print texts. The goal is to improve their willingness and ability to engage and to help them develop literacy skills that include fluency, word knowledge, and comprehension.

Entering Text activities give students the opportunity to explore portions of text before reading an entire chapter or selection. All students participate in the interpretation processes. Everyone may be called on to represent text physically and to describe what the text means to them. These activities promote repeated practice and ownership of the ideas behind the words. By working with manageable selections such as words, phrases, or short paragraphs, struggling readers gain a sense of confidence. Above all, students are inspired to want to read by provoking curiosity about the content of the material.

In the "Insiders and Outsiders" unit, Bobby, Kevin, and the students explored questions like: "How is belonging to a group a good thing? A bad thing? Do we spend more time with people who are similar or different to us? Do we have a responsibility to leave a group or 'snitch' on them when they do something we disagree with? How far does loyalty go?" As the unit progressed, Bobby posed these questions during their classroom discussions and listened carefully as students illustrated their responses with personal stories. As Bobby explained, "During these conversations Russell appeared to be listening but didn't participate." When Bobby encouraged him, "Russell, would you like to add something to the conversation?" he shook his head. When Kevin next visited, he gave the students small portions of text from *The Outsiders*. He asked the students, in groups, to use their bodies to create statues or tableaus that illustrated various scenes (see chapter 3's "For the Classroom"). This time, Russell sat in the back row, far from the stage. Again, Kevin and Bobby let him be. Students formed tableaus; then with Kevin's encouragement, the groups explained the situation they were presenting, answered questions about their interpretive choices, and discussed how they might make their tableaus even better. Kevin encouraged, "For our final performance, we'll combine sections of *The Outsiders* with your own stories. You have amazing stories to tell. I loved hearing them. Everyone else in the community will love hearing them as well. Our job over the next few weeks is to tell our stories as best we can so they will live on in ways that others will remember and learn from."

Even before the students began to read the book, Kevin and Bobby helped them establish connections to its themes. They knew the students struggled with reading but believed that by exploring some of the critical questions and themes taken up in *The Outsiders,* they could provide a bridge between the students' lived experience and the world portrayed in the novel. By explaining that the students were to tell their stories in a final performance, Kevin established a concrete goal for the class to work toward. He knew that at times the process would be difficult. He knew there would be days where the energy would flag. He saw the possibility that students other than Russell might choose not to participate. Yet, he could point to the need to prepare for a performance as a reason to keep working through problems that might arise.

COMPREHENDING TEXT

Once a student establishes purposes for reading, develops interest in addressing a question or satisfying a curiosity, and is introduced to its language, she is prepared to engage in a dialogue with text. The point of Comprehending Text work is for students to engage deeply with print. For students to comprehend, they must decode written symbols fluently and automatically and have a sufficient degree of word knowledge to construct meaning. Further, they must maintain focus and exercise stamina. Once a person becomes a proficient reader, the techniques and processes used become automatic and largely invisible. To the nonproficient reader, they remain a mystery.

Students vary widely in the amount of reading they do both in and out of school. Middle school–age children who read very little read an average of 100,000 words annually. Avid readers read as many as 10 million words a year. This represents a 100:1 differential.[15] To put it another way, the amount of time children at the tenth percentile spend reading outside of school each year amounts to just two days of reading for the child at the ninetieth percentile.[16] The growth of the Internet and other forms of electronic communications may be changing what it means to read, as is our understanding and the core definition of reading. Still, the point remains: a wide variation exists in the time and type of reading students do.

Increasingly, educators have begun to design instruction around specific strategies that support, or *scaffold,* students as they become skilled readers. Many scripted curricula introduce students to practices such as predicting, questioning, inferring, visualizing. Strategy instruction offers a great improvement over more laissez-faire "assign and test" approaches used in the past. Working with a range of comprehension strategies benefits students more than round-robin reading, a ubiquitous but questionable activity in which students take turns reading aloud to the entire class small segments of text they are encountering for the first time. By working with a repertoire of alternate strategies that help them focus, practice, read, think, talk, and write, students become better able to make and share hypotheses, seek and share evidence, and offer interpretations. Yet those strategies benefit students most when they perceive them as closely tied to personal and social goals. Often as they introduce and practice reading strategies, teachers emphasize the *how* and forget to establish the *why.*

Louise Rosenblatt wrote thoughtfully about why people read.[17] She described a reader's *stance,* or what we pay attention to, as a continuum. On one end of the continuum, an *efferent* reading pays more attention to factual, analytic, logical, and quantitative aspects of a text. On the other end, an *aesthetic* reading pays more attention to the sensuous, affective, emotive, and qualitative aspects. Skilled, committed readers may take either or both stances. The nature of the text, the background and interests of the reader, and the circumstances of the reading create the *transaction* between reader and text. By linking comprehension to performance, the transaction becomes visible, public, and open for discussion.

Informal performances of small segments of text help students to focus and read carefully and analytically. Students may read aloud with partners, in small groups, or chorally; they may rehearse by repeating readings. Their purposeful and repeated engagement with text helps to increase their focus and stamina and ultimately their comprehension. The emphasis is not on error but on growth. Students engage in a dialogue among self, text, and community.

Bobby chose *The Outsiders* for his students to read because of its relevance to their lives. He explained, "What a perfect book for these kids. *The Outsiders* is real. Hinton wrote the book because she couldn't find books about the teenagers she knew. And she was fifteen years old. My kids loved that a teenager wrote it and it didn't pull any punches."[18] He knew that this text would allow many opportunities in class for discussing themes that were relevant to the lived experience of the students. While reading *The Outsiders,* Bobby's class discussed questions about relationships, loyalties, and friendship. They discussed the actions of the characters in the novel and their feelings about those actions. They read for an authentic purpose—not to complete worksheets and take tests but, rather, to reflect on their own experiences, to write their own stories. By connecting the text to their own experience, they widened their horizons, deepened their comprehension, and acknowledged the authority of texts to contribute to their understanding of the world.

CREATING TEXT

When students, inspired by their reading, begin to create responses, their work is often filled with what Walt Whitman called "original energy." In Maxine Greene's words, they connect their lives and the larger world and "imagine it could be otherwise."[19] Obviously, at times it's appropriate for teachers to seek accuracy, correctness, and precision through efferent readings. However, it's equally appropriate to encourage and invite surprise, not knowing how a student will answer a question or what stories he has to tell. Valuable and beautiful stories exist in the lives of students in our classrooms. By inviting students to create text, the curriculum honors their ideas and voices.

To create a final performance, students combine their own work with portions of the core text. Their writing may take the form of a play script, poetry, analytical essay, personal narrative, or fiction. Writing may be *personal*, connecting the content of the text to students' lives; *analytical*, critiquing the core text; *aesthetic*, using the text as a platform for inspiring artful response; or *associative*, comparing the central text to other texts or events occurring in the world beyond the text. Students may respond by using other symbol systems: a short film, a dance, a series of drawings or other types of visual art, or music. Whatever forms the new texts take, by creating them, students explore spaces around an assigned text, provide an interpretation, or place the text in a wider context.

Creating Text assignments may either be specific and focused or open-ended, with room for interpretation and creative response. Through establishing an environment of possibility, students "talk back to text." They recognize that they have the power to influence the world around them by creating responses that have an immediate audience in the classroom and even in the larger community. Students use this component of the Performance Cycle to advance their understanding of the core text, thus offering something new to the world.

Inspired by the literature they heard and read, Bobby's students wrote stories about being insiders and outsiders. Everyone, including Russell, has stories that are waiting to be told. To assist them, the teacher introduced storyboards. Dividing a piece of paper into several squares, he asked the students to draw a picture in each square representing the progression of their story. Then his students wrote sentences that described each picture. Bobby added layers to the writing process: "Does anyone talk in the story? Let's add that. I want to hear what they say."

When Kevin visited, he asked students to read their dialogue and then act it out on the stage. Russell still didn't step up to the stage, but by this point he was sitting next to Kevin in the front row of the auditorium. After students practiced the dialogue, they created tableaus that matched their storyboards. As they performed, Kevin quietly turned to Russell and pointed to one of the group's tableaus, asking, "What do you think? Is it good? How could they make it better?" Quietly, Russell offered suggestions. Finally, Kevin said to the students on the stage, "Russell has some ideas about your sculpture. Do you mind?" As Russell began to explain, Kevin encouraged him: "Russell, why don't you get up on stage and show them what you're talking about?" He did.

REVISING/REHEARSING TEXT

One of the hardest things for teachers to do is to convince students to revisit and revise their work in a serious and meaningful way. Teachers customarily point out to students the value of practice as a means of improving any skill. They demand. They cajole. They structure assignments to build revision into the process. Students often find ways around the teachers' expectations and assignment. Logic is on the students' side, since their interest in the topic and the assignment is often limited to receiving a passing grade.

As teachers and artists, we know that serious and accomplished creators in every discipline hone and polish their work carefully and consistently. Creating high-quality work in any field requires patience, attention to detail, and time. American culture today—adolescent culture in particular— is a culture of immediacy. The instant feedback derived from video games or the excitement of fast-paced action movies often contrasts with the skills required to create high-quality work. Excellent writing and excellent performance both demand multiple drafts. Revision and rehearsal are key skills teachers have the opportunity to teach explicitly through the Performance Cycle.

When performances are presented to a real audience for a real purpose, students are more likely to take the quality of their performance seriously and craft and shape their work with great care. For many students, engaging in the Performance Cycle from initial design to final performance in front of a real audience may make a substantive difference in the seriousness with which they approach their work.

Revising and rehearsing are key habits students need to develop. In preparing a performance, students give and receive feedback on their own and each others' work. They self-assess. Teachers weigh in. Productive feedback from peers and others enables students to elevate the quality of their work.[20]

In preparing to perform, the students produced a series of drafts. First, they told their stories orally. Then they created tableaus of critical moments in their stories. They discussed their stories, then drew storyboards. They translated their storyboards into writing and added descriptions and dialogues. In turning their stories into performances, the students revisited their writing to revise, refine, and reshape the work. Kevin added a narrator to each story, and the students heard their entire stories read by others. As they listened to their stories being read, each student sat next to Kevin with pen and paper in hand. In the role of playwright, they made changes in the narration or dialogue. Knowing they would be presenting their stories to an audience, they listened intently. They crossed out, erased, added, or changed words and lines, trying to get it right.

PERFORMING TEXT

Ask adults to describe the school experience in which they remember being the most *academically awake*. Often the example will describe a performance of some sort, something built or created, a speech, a written piece usually for an audience other than the teacher. When students engage in the work of Performing Text, they use their reading, writing, and critical thinking skills.

In contrast to traditional school theater programs, ArtsLiteracy students do not perform a play in its entirety. Performances include combining student work in a range of symbol systems with selections from the original text. At its most productive, a performance addresses one or more questions established at the outset of the process. ArtsLiteracy teachers often supplement their students' final performances with written assignments. A test is not a suitable substitute for a performance. The point is to create a rich and memorable experience that prepares students to respond successfully to a wide range of assessments.

The performance may occur within one classroom, in front of a group of peers or younger children, or in a full-blown production in a high-stakes environment. Performance provides a concrete goal for everyone to work toward, and the reality of presenting one's work to an authentic audience engenders high-quality work.[21] When students perform in front of an audience, they acquire genuine responsibilities and take risks—behaviors adolescents value.[22] Performances embed literacy in a larger purpose. Students read and write at least in part because they know in a few weeks or months they will be in front of an audience performing their own work. The challenge of performance brings a sense of shared purpose, solidifies relationships within the learning community, and establishes motives for future community efforts and endeavors.[23]

The risks Russell and his fellow students took to mount the stage and perform were numerous. They had never before performed in front of an audience. Since they were in a self-contained classroom, they rarely even spent time with the rest of the students in the school, and they were worried about what others might think. Despite these challenges—or perhaps because of them—they presented a stunning performance in the school's auditorium in the presence of their families, friends, and teachers.

The performance began with a tableau of the two groups of youth represented in *The Outsiders,* the Greasers and the Socs. One by one, the students came onto the stage, recited a line spoken by one of the characters, and froze in a pose. By the end of the opening, the students were all frozen, the Greasers on one side of the stage and the Socs on the other. Following this initial tableau, the students acting out an individual story. The performance continued to move between scenes from the novel and stories from the students' lives.

The education director of the Tony Award–winning Trinity Repertory Company observed from the audience. She invited the group to perform on the theater's main stage complete with professional lighting and sound in an evening that featured student performances from around Rhode Island. At Trinity, Russell confidently stepped onto the stage, said his line—"Things are rough all over"—and struck a pose. Once again the students presented tableaus portraying the Socs and Greasers. And once again they wove together their own stories of being insiders and outsiders with portions of Hinton's memorable novel. After the performance, we heard Russell say the same words that have been offered by many students over the years: "When can we do that again?"

REFLECTION

From five-minute activities to full days of classroom work, reflection is at the heart of the Performance Cycle. As we define it, reflection is the act of looking back at the work done by both individuals and groups. It encompasses reviewing the content learned, the processes of one's own mind, and the learning of the entire group. We identify reflection with the development of the capacity for *mindfulness* and see reflective practice as a means of ensuring that teachers, artists, and students consistently discuss their work. By highlighting successes and areas for improvement, they make visible and explicit what everyone in the community is learning.[24]

In the ArtsLiteracy Project, debriefing discussions occur frequently at the end of an activity, a class, or a final performance. One common form of reflection is the *talk-back,* when performers address questions posed by audience members. At their most successful, these sessions illuminate what participants have learned about both the content and the process of preparing and presenting a performance.

Other forms ask individuals to talk or write about their learning, using their capacity for metacognition, or thinking about thinking, to assess their development. Cognitive neuroscientist Andy Clark identifies metacognition as "a cluster of powerful capacities involving self-evaluation, self criticism and finely honed remedial responses . . . The process of linguistic formulation creates the stable structure to which subsequent thinkings attach." Clark explains, "It is because we can think about our own thinking that we can actively structure our world in ways designed to promote, support, and extend our own cognitive achievements."[25]

Yet another reflective approach invites individuals to comment on the efforts and achievements of the group by describing their thoughts about the environment and the process and content of the collective effort. Reflection helps students to think about their work, develop self-knowledge and acquire a perspective on the broader learning environment.

Providing time and space for reflection gives students and teachers alike the opportunity to evaluate their own growth. Education at its essence is about the development of the human being and the community. Without a reflective space, we rush from task to task perhaps not realizing how individual moments add up to a whole. When we reflect on both the process and content of our work, we're better able to see our own learning as well as the larger learning environment and consider how both might be improved.

After the *Insiders and Outsiders* performance, Bobby asked his students to participate in a talk-back with the audience. From the apron of the stage, students took questions and encouraged students in the audience to respond to what they had just seen. Back in the classroom, Bobby and his students often discussed the performance over the course of the year. So, for example, when Russell came to class with an attitude or low energy, Bobby said, "Remember you in that performance at Trinity? Remember you up on stage underneath the bright lights? This isn't the Russell we know. Can someone tell me what Russell was like on stage?" And the reflection began again.

SUMMARY

In his excellent book *Imagination in Teaching and Learning,* Kieran Egan describes the characteristics of young adolescents' imaginative lives. Because each human being is "essentially a story-telling animal," and "the role of story is fundamental to our sense-making," Egan argues for narrative as the most effective form of teaching and learning.[26] Young adolescents, he contends, find compelling the exploration of big themes such as extremes and limits, romance, wonder and awe, association with the heroic, revolt, and idealism. Across the curriculum, topics presented in this form encourage students to explore them not as fixed systems to be comprehended but as possible worlds to be investigated and shaped.

The arts invite us to use multiliteracies in all their dimensions—oral, written, kinesthetic, musical, and visual. All art forms contain powerful symbol systems for making and communicating meaning.[27] As human beings, we want to speak and we want to listen. Literacy is essentially about this communicative give and take. When we create genuine literacy experiences with our students, we leave room to develop a shared understanding and to convey the unexpected. If we offer texts that are both meaningful and challenging and provide a space for students to tell their stories, the community receives gifts we never would have imagined. The Performance Cycle invites us all—teachers, students, and community alike—to use the power of the arts to learn and grow.

In summary, the Performance Cycle:

- Builds a positive community of practice in the classroom
- Creates a purpose and focus for learning
- Provides a framework for a curriculum that is purposeful, inquiry centered, and activity based and is carefully crafted to meet the needs of specific students in specific classrooms
- Promotes students' receptivity or openness to working with print text
- Uses a wide range of multiliteracies
- Promotes oral and print literacy skills, including reading, writing, speaking, and listening
- Makes print texts compelling and comprehensible through embodying or bringing them to life
- Allows for explicitness in modeling and instruction
- Makes participants' thinking about text visible for others to learn from, question, critique, etc.
- Leads to a final performance of understanding for real audiences and real purposes
- Establishes a context for metacognition, self-regulatory behavior, and mindfulness.

Several years after the *Insider and Outsider* performance, Russell's class was collaborating with three other classes on a performance project called *Talking Walls of Central Falls,* which included dance, murals, performance, and photography. In an early rehearsal, the director reviewed the structure of the final performance for all the students. He announced, "Scene 8 is Russell's story." Russell's teacher asked, "Shall we edit it? Do some cutting?" The director responded, "No. I want to use the whole thing. But Russell, you need to find three other people to do this scene with you and have it ready in four weeks." Russell, focused on the director, nodded and responded. "No problem."

2

Building Community in Schools and Classrooms

Classroom as Ensemble

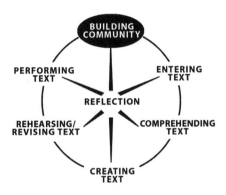

[In Daniel's class] everybody gets a family, friends, a house, trust, and courage to live.

—Mateus Rodrigues, a student in Daniel Soares's class

THE CORDEL

WHEN DANIEL SOARES walked into his classroom in Inhumas, Brazil, one morning, his high school–age students were intently discussing a murder that had occurred the previous night.

"Where exactly did it happen?"

"On the side of the lake near the bars and the street."

The city had recently constructed a walking path around the only lake in Inhumas. In an area with few parks, the lake served as a community center, a place to socialize and exercise at all hours of the day. The violence had occurred beside this lake, right in the heart of Inhumas.

After the students had established the details of the story, their conversation turned to conditions in Inhumas. In the past six months, the small city of fifty thousand residents located near the capital city of Brasilia had witnessed twenty-five murders.

"What's going on? Why aren't the police doing anything?"

"I can't believe this is happening in our city. Inhumas has always been a peaceful place."

"The police aren't doing anything. It feels like no one is doing anything."

There was a moment of silence. Then, one student spoke up, "We should dress up and make a protest in the town square."

"Dress up how?" Daniel asked.

"Why don't we make a cordel around the lake? It can be a cordel for peace. We'll use poems that we've read in class and add our own poems to it," a student suggested.

As a Fulbright Scholar in the United States, Daniel Soares had spent considerable time working with the ArtsLiteracy Project. Returning to his home country, he continued his ArtsLiteracy work, merging aspects of the Performance Cycle with familiar local traditions. In his school in Inhumas, Daniel began to use elements of the traditional practice of creating a cordel as a way for his students to share their writing. *Literatura de cordel,* Portuguese for "string literature," has a long history in Brazil. Cordels are strings stretched between two posts in markets or town squares used to display *folhetos,* small inexpensive chapbooks containing long narrative poems and illustrations.[1]

Daniel's students read poetry in both Portuguese and English, often translating the poems from one language to another. Every day they read and discussed at least one poem and then wrote poems of their own. At the end of class, students read their work to one another and posted some on the cordel in the hallway for others to read. Requiring only paper, pencil, clothesline, and clothespins, the cordel offered a simple way to publish their writing. This display, Daniel found, was motivating to the authors and inspiring to others. Always a work in progress, writing on the cordel was constantly being taken down, revised, hung back up, and performed. Traditionally, in the marketplace, cordel authors read their work aloud. "The poet uses these opportunities to demand the public's wavering attention. He may summarize the story for those who have just joined the group or make humorous comparison between the tale and an event in daily life."[2] Daniel's students performed their writing in front of their cordel. Reading aloud in the school hallways, they called out to others walking by, adding humorous, improvisational asides, just as cordel authors do in the markets.

Frustrated with their city's lack of response to the murder, the students in Daniel's class decided to act. They felt a responsibility to face the recent violence with a show of unity and decided to build a peace cordel to surround the town's lake to display poems, stories, and essays expressing their feelings about the murders. Despite their initial excitement for the project, Daniel's students alone could never have completed it. It became immediately clear that such a large cordel would require citywide support. As Daniel explained, "We started to calculate how big the lake is, what we needed, how much cord we needed to buy, and we realized to do it all around the lake, we needed 5,000–6,000 pieces of paper, but we didn't have time to make all those papers. Impossible. What to do?"[3] The class considered the scope of the problem and realized they would need to ask other students for support. In Daniel's words:

We had to go to almost every school in the city. We went at least to every public school . . . We spent two weeks going to visit every class, talking about violence, what they thought about violence, and what they would like to tell the city about violence. So all these elementary students and high school students made a painting, wrote sentences or wrote a letter or poem, anything connected to violence. People took quotes from songs. And they all made this, and we had more than 6,000 pieces of paper we hung around the lake.[4]

Inspired by the poems they had been reading in class and guided by a collective purpose, Daniel's students visited classrooms throughout Inhumas to propose their project and solicit student work. The completed cordel thus became a true display of the power of the Inhumas community. Many students in the class knew or were related to someone who had recently been killed. They wrote not only out of a sense that their work would be read publicly but also out of a shared goal, using their words to change the course of future events.

WHEN THE STONES TALK

It was a Thursday evening. The sky around the lake, lit by the setting sun, displayed deep purples, pinks, and blues. A cordel stretched around the entire lake, the pages blowing in the breeze. Daniel explained,

We invited the mayor. The vice mayor was there. The judge was there. The radio was there. The newspaper was there. All the schools came; priests came; pastors came; everybody came. They made prayers. We made a march around the lake for peace. And the cordel was there for two days so people could see, and many people saw it; many people talked about it. Visually it was beautiful. The sun was setting. It reflected on the water.[5]

Throughout the afternoon and evening, family, friends, and strangers gathered to walk around the lake to read the words of the young people from their community. The students offered them pens and paper, encouraging them to join in. A mother took the writing tools from her son and went off alone to sit and write a poem, which she added to the cordel. Throughout the day, the words of the students mixed with the words of the older generation. Occasionally a student called for attention and read his poem to a small group gathered around him. The day had a strange calm to it, almost a meditative feel, as people came to read and write.

Later, when we asked if the cordel affected the incidence of violence in the community, he responded:

> This year we have less. I would not be presumptuous to say, "Oh, it was because of the cordel." I know the cordel made people talk about it. I know the mayor was at the radio talking about the violence. And the guy from the radio, he said something very interesting: "It has happened in Inhumas what the Bible says, if you don't talk, the stones have to talk." So it was necessary for the kids from schools to talk, so the mayor could do something.
>
> The mayor didn't like what he said, so he went to the radio, and I know we got some new cars for the police. I wouldn't say it was because of the cordel but because of the things we did, not only the cordel but because we went to the schools and talked to the students, and because we invited kids of five, six, seven, eight, nine years old. So the conversation became huge in the city, and after that we had much fewer deaths. I haven't heard of a person who died this year because of the drug issues.[6]

In performing the work they'd created for the cordel, the students started a conversation where before there had been only frustrating silence. The discussion incited action and decreased violence in the community. All this was made possible after the community came together for a purpose, united like the supportive cord surrounding their lake.

The cordel in Brazil may seem far removed from schools here in the United States. Yet, one year later, when a student was murdered in the small town of Central Falls, Rhode Island, arts teacher Deanna Camputaro worked with her students to create a cordel around the local high school, modeled after the one in Inhumas. In Rhode Island, students wrote text on long pieces of cloth and attached them to a clothesline. As the cloth blew in the breeze, a cellist sat at the front door of the school and played a solo in mourning.

THE CLASSROOM COMMUNITY

To create their powerful cordel projects, students in Inhumas, Brazil, and in Central Falls, Rhode Island, needed to rely on their communities. In schools as they presently exist, our emphasis is largely on the progress of single individuals. What are Samantha's SAT scores? What is her grade point average? How is her writing? Why is she not attending school? What colleges will she apply to? Although these are important questions, we pay less attention to questions about the classroom or community as a whole. Do we consider how, as members of a school community, we interact with one another?

When classroom activities focus on "covering" the textbook, completing end-of-chapter assignments, and taking tests, little or no opportunity exists to build a sense of classroom community. The culture of a class all too often becomes one of put-downs and name calling, with students disrespecting each other and the teacher. When we first began the ArtsLiteracy Project, we were surprised to find that often, even midway through a school year, students in classes together did not know each other's names. These observations led us to pay attention to the characteristics of classroom communities and the role they play in supporting students' literacy development. We decided to focus on building purposeful and supportive classroom communities as the initial step in our work, a step that we have come to believe is essential especially for secondary school students who have yet to see the connection between classroom literacy activities and their own identities and personal goals.

Most literacy programs begin directly with asking students to comprehend an assigned text. This is an understandable aim. For students to improve as readers and writers, they need to read closely and widely, both extensively and intensively. They must reach a point of fluency in which they can, in Nancie Atwell's words, lose themselves in "the reading zone" and begin to "live vicariously in books."[7] However, our work, along with that of many others, has shown that the characteristics of a person's social world play a major part in her identity development and the activities she chooses.[8] For students to become members of what Frank Smith describes as "the literacy club," they must see the club as a community that welcomes and supports them and where they can make a significant contribution.[9] For students to be willing to take the risks involved in talking about difficult issues, a strong community must develop in individual classrooms and in the school as a whole. In such a literacy community, students share books with each other, discuss how these books relate to their lives, analyze and perform stories and poems, and create new artistic work.

A community forms as students participate in exhibitions and performances like the cordel project in Brazil. While icebreakers and warm-ups (see "For the Classroom") create a positive environment, a more substantial community is established and persists when the group moves beyond these activities to create meaningful work to share with an audience. In the best circumstances, learning experiences are characteristic of an entire school culture. In a classroom community, all members share a collective purpose; feel that they belong, have a voice, and are visible; and collaborate to create original work.

SHARED PURPOSE

When students in Inhumas and Central Falls were surrounded by violence in their communities, they responded with cordels of poems and stories. They knew their reading and writing was purposeful, and their purpose bound them together as a literacy community. In Brazil, Daniel brought poems and poetry books into the classroom. Students searched the Internet for songs and poems that spoke to the tragedies they were experiencing in their town. Guided by a shared purpose, they wrote their own responses, exchanged writing, peer edited each other's work, and gathered in groups to plan the details of the cordel event. Every day when Daniel asked if any students had writing to share, several hands went up. Students felt proud of their work and were eager to perform for one another and for a larger audience.

Over the years, we have seen many similar purposeful literacy communities develop in classrooms. In ArtsLiteracy classrooms at Brown Summer

High School, a month-long summer lab school on the campus of Brown University, students know from the outset that their course will culminate with a public performance. Parents, friends, and teachers watch students perform their interpretations and original responses to a classic novel, play, or collection of short stories or poetry. Preparing for these performances gives classrooms a shared sense of purpose. Though these students are by no means skilled—or even prospective—performers, everyone knows they are working toward something real. The students know that at the end of the program they will perform in front of a live audience, and this awareness motivates everyone to collaborate. Students create the performance. They help design the final production and figure out how to produce it. Students become participants rather than passive receivers of information.

Indeed, performance is a democratizing process that makes educational opportunities possible to a wide range of learning styles. A performance both extends a community's boundaries and deepens participants' engagement as they work together toward their shared purpose. Students with the potential to be skilled performers may be labeled "failures" in school. Traditional modes of teaching in the fields of both literacy and numeracy are often ineffective for young people like Russell, the student whose story we tell in the previous chapter. For them, a request to participate in any sort of academic activity may seem like an occasion for failure, so they choose not to participate rather than fail again. When they participate successfully in a performance that uses the skills they bring to an environment, they want to repeat this success. They have created high-quality work, and they want to do it again.

Educator Ted Sizer imagines schools as places where students share their work publicly on an ongoing basis. Sizer explains, "Exhibitions can be powerful incentives for students. Knowing where the destination is always helps in getting there, and if that destination is cast in an interesting way, one is more likely to care about reaching it."[10] The cordel project—or exhibition—represented a collective destination that was developed and implemented jointly by students and teachers. In other exhibitions, like those in Brown Summer High School and other classrooms, the teacher may establish the destination and then draw on students' skills to contribute, shape, tune, and sharpen the work as they move toward that culminating event. In both cases, knowing the direction in which they are moving helps the class stay motivated to arrive.

BELONGING

In a literacy community with a shared focus, every single person contributes. Teachers and artists learn what students can offer, and then they modify or alter the direction of the work based on students' interests, skills, and talents. As Daniel's student Mateus put it, "Everybody gets a family, friends, a house, trust, and courage to live."[11] This student's use of *family motifs* reflects a feeling of belonging in school that is critical to student success. Researcher Sonia Nieto explains:

> Building on family motifs, that is, on the values, traditions, and talents at the heart of a family, can be used in the service of education. Although many families of all backgrounds face tremendous challenges and negative situations, positive virtues can be found in almost all families, and using them can make the classroom an environment in which all children feel a sense of belonging. Failing to do so perpetuates the message that not everybody belongs there.[12]

As Nieto points out, one of the most important aspects of family is a sense of belonging. In creating the cordel with Daniel in Brazil, all students played a role and felt they were part of a family. Everyone had at least one piece of writing displayed on the cordel. Each took part in planning the event—designing invitations, mapping out the space, directing the performance, constructing the cordel—and interacted with community members on the day of the event. Students' participation connected them to one another. In a classroom that was working *toward* something, they all felt part of something larger than themselves.

Unfortunately, as Nieto writes, "the significance of 'family' in the education of children often is overlooked by schools."[13] The culture of standardized testing emphasizes the sorting and ranking of students. Reducing student performance to a set of numbers does little to inspire a sense of connectedness and often ignores the significance of students' cultural backgrounds. This, in turn, makes school feel like an alien place. Currently, our education system faces the challenge of finding a balance between establishing and measuring standards in academic achievement and creating inclusive and welcoming school and classroom communities.

A sense of belonging to a learning community encourages students and teachers to interact in genuine ways and to gain respect for the resources each brings to the project. We are often surprised by the variety of previously unknown skills students reveal. In one class we learned that a student was a beautiful flamenco dancer. She offered to dance in a performance of the class's response to Garcia Lorca's play *Blood Wedding*.[14] She enlisted her boyfriend, who played classical Spanish guitar, and their piece became the highlight of the performance. The shared goal of their learning community allowed these students to showcase a skill that they had never before exhibited in a classroom environment.

In almost every class we encounter students who like to build things by working with materials such as wood, fabric, or paint. In the typical classroom, these students may sit quietly in the background. When they are able to contribute to a community effort, their valuable talents emerge and they come alive. After such experiences, students feel more at home inside the classroom. Their desire and ability to work on assignments is then likely to increase. For them, the classroom has become a supportive environment, a place where they are willing to take risks, a community to which they belong.

VISIBILITY

Theater director Augusto Boal is the originator of an approach called Forum Theatre in which he reimagines the role of the audience as *spectactors*.[15] In this method, a professional theater troupe presents a scene that often illustrates a contentious situation in a community. In a community with a labor conflict, for instance, the troupe begins with a scene about the factory owners and the laborers. Audience members may stop the scene at any time, walk on the stage, and become an actor, changing the arc of the play and its outcome. In this powerful paradigm shift, the audience no longer sits quietly, passively, watching the drama unfold but, rather, has the power to become visible, to change the course of action.

Boal's invitation to the audience allows spectators to assume center stage to act in a situation that matters to their community. In establishing a community of literacy learners, teachers can create a similar shift. Students perform their responses to texts, making their learning and their levels of engagement visible. This exposure might initially be very off-putting to students like Russell, who are accustomed to hiding behind the many sorts of curtains they create to protect themselves in the classroom. However, when passive observers realize their potential as actors within their community, the result for students and Boal's spect-actors alike is highly empowering. Students often conceal themselves behind their own curtains. Some hide their struggles with reading and writing. Some hide from engaging intellectually with one another. Others hide emotionally. A student's difficulties with literacy can remain hidden in the curtain of labels like "conduct disorder" or "attention deficit disorder."

The multidimensional nature of the arts makes student literacy in the classroom visible. In the process of learning to display their understanding of challenging texts, students become active members of a community where they are more fully known to one another and to their teachers. Classrooms have the potential to be richly textured places where laughter and play provide a critical part of student learning.

Literacy educators like Emilia Ferreiro and Louise Rosenblatt describe the transactions with text that ordinarily happen—or, for students who have difficulty, ordinarily don't happen—in the mind of individual readers.[16] By making this process visible through work in the arts, students share diverse interpretations and help one another develop as readers in a social environment. As educator Jeffrey Wilhelm explains, drama is "a way of bringing the invisible secrets of engaged readers out into the open" to be "observed and shared and tried on by other readers."[17] We see the power of a community of readers that develops as students actively share interpretations through multiple modalities. When a shared sense of support and mutual respect are present, students' ideas and interpretations become visible to one another and to the larger community as well.

CREATING

Too often in classrooms, we show students a predetermined product and say, directly or indirectly, "This is an A. If done right, your presentation/essay/ poem/lab report will look like this." While such an approach may prove useful and sometimes necessary, the search for the right answer limits students' development as critical thinkers and leaves them ill-prepared for the world they are about to enter, a world of problems lacking obvious answers or predetermined solutions. Rarely in the world do we encounter a set of tasks with clear, easy answers. Rather, we face a series of complex, evolving problems that we must, together with our community, work our way through. While mastering a body of factual information often provides a foundation for appropriately addressing issues or problems, learners absorb that information best when they understand its relevance to the issues they face.

In classrooms, it is common to see students working in groups. Groups may be assigned to collaborate on a problem set in algebra, complete a lab in chemistry, or answer multiple-choice questions about a short story in English. Yet, these activities often do not demand the kinds of social and cognitive skills required when team members truly give of themselves to creatively address a problem, suggest a solution, or formulate an innovation.

A community flourishes when everyone in the classroom, including the teacher, undertakes a shared journey of creation, thus progressing toward a common goal. Crucially, however, community members need to be open to the creative process along the way and therefore need *not* to rely on achieving any predetermined outcome or replicating someone else's model. Paolo Freire refers to this experience, the openness to create something original, as *ruptura* and describes it as breaking from the past and entering a new space. "In fact, however, there is no creativity without *ruptura*, without a break from the old, without conflict in which you have to make a decision. I would say there is no human existence without *ruptura*."[18] Rather than striving individually to produce the right answer, students in a strong classroom community work as members of a team, building on—or breaking from—past models to experience the creative process and produce their own innovative work together.

THE COMMUNITY-LITERACY CONNECTION

Forming school advisory groups, developing school mission statements that contain words like *respect* and *safe space*, or engaging in initial warm-up activities all constitute valid ways to begin building a school community. A truly vital community forms, however, when students and teachers feel they have accomplished something real and significant together. *Building Community* is the first segment of the Performance Cycle. We have come to see community as a fundamental component of student literacy development, a component that provides the foundation for subsequent phases like entering and comprehending text. However, our pedagogical model is, crucially, a *cycle*. As you continue to read this book, you will find that the other components of the Performance Cycle are essential for building community, too. When we wrestle with a text and share ideas and stories, we create new work, and when we perform for parents and peers, we deepen our community. In the shared movement toward something larger than ourselves, community is formed and continually strengthened.

Much like a professional theater company, the Performance Cycle closes with a performance. A professional theater group begins with building an ensemble. Actors work together and grow as a cast to create a performance. After the show, however, they go their separate ways to find another show and another cast. The Performance Cycle is different. When students in a class perform together for an audience, they create community. At this point, a performance establishes a foundation for deep literacy learning. A vital community not only provides the first step in supporting and encouraging the creative process but also functions as the *product* of this process. Performing displays what the community has achieved and thus affirms the strength of the bonds formed. In a sense, when the residents of Inhumas displayed their cordel, they were not only showcasing their art but also their unity.

Initially, the project seemed far too big for Daniel's students to embark on alone. When they worked as members of a team, however, they were able to create a cordel that surrounded the lake, the heart of their community. The string, which at first hung empty in the air, became a showcase of poems, photographs, and stories, and the cordel grew. Students took their work down, revised it, and hung new versions. The cordel evolved, as did the students in the classroom as new talents, skills, and interests surfaced. In this effort, individuals formed and displayed their originality on the strength of string connecting them in a shared goal.

In the year following the cordel project, Daniel taught the same group of students. "The group I had last year are my students this year, and they are unbelievably great in my classes. What's really cool is that after the cordel, we really started to have a sense of friendship and community, which really helps today."[19] The strong sense of community that develops following a performance leads us to recommend that teachers create performances with their students as early as possible in their time together. This sense of community creates an essential foundation for students to engage in reading and writing in powerful and meaningful ways.

To build classroom communities, we've drawn on activities developed by arts educators, including Greg Atkins, Augusto Boal, Dorothy Heathcote, Jennifer Wolf, Jan Mandell, Michael Rohd, Viola Spolin, and Ruth Zapporah.[20] We open classes or workshops by asking students to use their voices and bodies in a range of exercises and games. Students are out of their seats and on their feet communicating with one other. These activities awaken students and help to create a classroom culture of mutual care and support. They merge movement and language in ways that provide an impetus for students' literacy development.

JahnMary Acosta, a student in an ArtsLiteracy class, describes it this way:

I remember when our actor first stepped into our class. He was so energetic and alive. We were gathered in a circle on stage, and there were instruments set aside. I knew that this man was up to no good. He wanted to break our silence and the comfortable cliques that we were in.

For a person like me, this was not a very good sign. For years I've been known as the shy kid, the intelligent one that always sits in her little corner. I built this wall around me that seemed so soothing, unaware of the excitement around me. I had given up on becoming an outspoken person, the leader. But now it was all about to change. Here I was standing in a circle with some crazy actor making us do all of these chants or "exercises."

He emphasized the word *ensemble*. "Now we must work as an ensemble in order to feel comfortable with each other. This way things run smoothly and everyone becomes a family." At this point everyone was giggling; it was as if we were in the first grade all over again. He would put on the most exaggerated facial expressions every time he said *ENSEMBLE*.

No one could believe that we would be standing here for a month doing these silly activities. "Now would everyone honor my gesture and repeat it in unison while saying my name." I know that everyone was probably thinking, "How can this help us on stage? This is so stupid and useless."

Who would have known that at the end of that school year not only would I be performing, but I would also teach my own class. All of those silly activities were able to break the shells that everyone had built around themselves. Now I have more friends than I would have asked for, and our class left united. We created our own community in which no one is frightened of performing or sharing anything personal. We have truly created a model of what a classroom should look like![21]

FOR THE CLASSROOM

BUILDING COMMUNITY

The section that follows describes classroom activities we developed—and in some cases learned from others—to support community building in the classroom. Each of the remaining chapters will conclude with a "For the Classroom" section that addresses its particular aspect of the Performance Cycle. For additional activities, see the Handbook pages of the ArtsLiteracy Web site, www.artsliteracy.org/Handbook.

Common Ground

Common ground is a way for group members to share background information strengths, abilities, and interests. Begin by creating an imaginary line across the length of the room, with half being the "yes" side and the other the "no" side. For younger students, it might be helpful to use tape to create an actual line and mark the sides. Gather everyone on the "no" side of the line. Call out questions such as "Do you play a musical instrument?" (See a list of possibilities below.) Students who play a musical instrument step to the "yes" side; the remainder stay on the "no" side. During the activity, you may request more details—for example, asking each student on the "yes" side to name the musical instrument he plays.

Initial prompts can explore the diversity of abilities and interests of the students:

- Do you speak more than one language?
- Do you sing?
- Do you dance?
- Do you write poetry or lyrics?
- Do you play a musical instrument?
- Have you traveled outside the United States?
- Do you have an afterschool job?

Prompts can then introduce themes that connect students' lives to a designated text. For instance, in preparing to read Ovid's myth of *Daedalus and Icarus*, you might offer the following prompts:

- Have you ever learned a craft from an adult?
- Have you ever done something risky you regretted later?
- Have you ever wished you could fly?

After you demonstrate Common Ground, students may generate their own prompts. We've often used students' responses to this activity later in preparing a culminating performance. We might ask students who write poetry if they'd like to perform their poems or students who play an instrument and write songs to compose and perform an opening song for the performance.

The Truth About Me

Students gather in the center of the space. One student who volunteers to step away from the group says, "The truth about me is . . ." and completes the phrase. For instance, "The truth about me is I like to go hiking." Everyone who shares that interest moves toward the student and forms a group around her. Another student steps out of the initial group and makes another statement: "The truth about me is I like the television series *The Sopranos*." One by one, students step out of the various groups that form around the room, stating new "truths" and forming new groups.

In a more structured variation, each student in the class receives a number. When you call out the student's number, he steps out of the group and gives his statement. Others who agree form a group with the speaker at the center.

In another variation, students form a large circle around the perimeter of the room. With a piece of masking tape, each student marks his spot on the floor. One student is left without a spot. That student stands in the center of the circle and makes a statement. All those who share the same truth move into the center of the circle and stand with the student. The student who made the statement calls out, "1, 2, 3, go!" and everyone runs to capture an empty spot. One student will be left without a spot. She then goes to the center and makes her statement. The activity continues.

Name and Gesture

Students gather in a large circle. As they say their names one by one, each creates a bold physical movement that represents some aspect of their personality. Begin the exercise by modeling, and then ask everyone to repeat your movement and name. (For example, Aliza throws her hands in the air and jumps at the same time, calling out "Aliza." The rest of the class then follows, throwing their hands up in the air and calling out "Aliza.") The next student then makes her own gesture while saying her name. Continue around the circle, always beginning with Aliza and repeating everyone's gesture and name as the new name is added. For this activity, instruct students to copy name and gesture as accurately as possible and with the same commitment. Encourage students to make bold choices and to make their physical movements large.

Variations on this include:

- *Alliteration.* Instruct students to choose an adjective that begins with the first letter of his name and use that in the game. For example: Magical Maria, Jubilant John.
- *Vocabulary.* Students may use a vocabulary or spelling word in place of their names and create a gesture that reflects the feeling or definition of that word.

The Human Atom

This simple movement activity represents the foundation of much of the ArtsLiteracy Project's work. The goal is to have students move around the room and participate in an assortment of activities that are listed below.

To begin, the group creates as wide open a space as possible, and students begin moving around the room, walking to the center, to the edge, to the center, to the edge. Suddenly the classroom atmosphere changes. People aren't seated in rows listening to one speaker. They are moving in space and eventually looking at and interacting with one another.

If creating an open space in the classroom is difficult, find a different space—the stage in the auditorium or a space in the cafeteria or a school hallway. Before leaving the classroom, be sure to create some clear behavioral guidelines with the students.

The basic activity is simple. Delineate a point at the center of the room and explain that this point is the "nucleus" for the activity. All of the students in the room are "electrons." They walk to the center of the nucleus, then to a far point in the room, back to the nucleus, and then back out to another far point in the room. Walking in this configuration ensures that students won't just walk in one continuous circle around the edge of the space. If you are working with just a few students, chairs or tape may be used to delineate a smaller space.

As a variation, ask students to picture a shape in their heads and imagine that shape taped onto the floor around the entire room. The students walk around the space following their imaginary shape.

As they walk, students do not speak. They listen for your instructions. They must avoid any physical contact unless it's part of the activity. As the activities progress, you "side coach," offering specific directions and reminders.

Next, choose among a series of activities, each one suggested by educators we've worked with and further developed by ArtsLiteracy Project staff. Some are adapted from the work of Shakespeare and Company, Augusto Boal, Jan Mandell, Magdalena Gómez, Liz Lerman's Dance Company, and Ruth Zaporah. Others we've developed in classrooms and workshop spaces. The activity's name, the Human Atom, was coined by Michael Baron, artistic director of the Lyric Theatre of Oklahoma.

Many teachers play music in the background to contribute to the energy of the activity, but the music shouldn't be recognizable to students or something they are likely to dance to. Our favorite tracks are from bassist Ernest Ranglin's recordings.

Human Atom Activities

• *Balance the space.* Everyone walks around the space. As they walk, they need to be aware of one another and work to balance the entire space, with no open areas, or groups of people walking together.

- *Ago/Ame.* Once students are out of their seats, on their feet, and moving, it's important to agree on some signals to call everyone to attention and direct activities. Jan Mandell uses a call-and-response approach drawn from a West African language. When she wants to call students to order, she calls out "Ago" (Are you listening?). Students then stop what they are doing, give her their attention, and respectfully respond, "Ame" (You have my attention). You may want to develop other signals to call for and hold students' attention.

- *Freeze.* Everyone learns to freeze on command. Students walk in the Human Atom formation, and when you say "freeze," everyone stops in place. No one moves any part of their bodies, including fingers and even eyes. By teaching the students to freeze, you will hold their attention as long as necessary to explain the next steps in the activity. It's likely that students will need to practice several times until they can remain still and silent. This is an essential skill to use later when the class begins to work with physical sculptures and tableaus.

- *Eye contact/Greeting.* As students walk, they make eye contact with everyone they see and offer a quick "hello." By greeting each other, students acknowledge that they are in a space together and will be working collaboratively and supportively over a period of time.

- *Friendship.* When students hear the word *friendship*, they introduce themselves to as many people as they can. You might also vary the speed of introductions by asking them to introduce themselves to each other "super-fast" or "super-slow." Remind them at "super-fast" to take care of each other while moving quickly around the space.

- *Freeze/Normal/Fast/Slow.* Ask the students to freeze. When they begin walking again, ask them to walk as fast as they can, still balancing the space and avoiding bumping into each other. Then have them freeze again. Now have them walk in slow motion. Freeze them again. Then let them choose to walk at normal speed, super-fast, super-slow, or remain frozen. Ask them to try different speeds.

- *Down/Up as ensemble.* As students walk, one person kneels. Then that person stands and another person kneels. At any moment, only one person in the entire group can be kneeling. The rest of the group continues to walk. The students need to feel the energy of the overall ensemble and decide when it is appropriate to kneel. At your direction, they experiment with two or three people kneeling at one time. After the students have mastered this collaboration, reverse the assignment. Everyone in the class will go down on one knee except one person who remains standing. This time only one person in the room can be up at a given moment. Then the students can practice having two or three people standing at one time. The idea is for the students to learn to work together as a group. If the students think only of themselves, the activity won't work. If two students begin to kneel at the same time, one must make way for the other. Each individual in the class must become aware of *all* members of the classroom community.

- *Forming shapes as ensemble.* The students begin by walking in the formation of the Human Atom. Instruct all of them to move into a perfect circle with everyone in the room and then freeze. They must do this in silence. At your instruction, they resume walking. Now direct them to create a square. Together and without talking, they form a square. Once they have it, they freeze. Continue to offer various prompts such as forming an equilateral triangle or a circle within a square.

- *Sculptures.* This activity is one of the easiest ways to introduce the idea of making statues or sculptures. It works very well after Freeze/Normal/Fast/Slow. At your command, students transform their entire bodies into sculptures. Ask them to freeze completely. Encourage students to create bold sculptures—low to the ground, high in the air—and eventually to connect their sculptures with one another. You can designate what the sculptures are to represent, or the students themselves can decide.

Activities in Pairs

For the following activities, students work in pairs. To create pairs, students walk in the Human Atom formation until you call out "back to back." The students quickly stand back-to-back with the person next to them and freeze. You then explain and model the activity to follow.

- *Stare down*. Explain, "Now face one another. Look into your partner's eyes as long as possible, without talking, and without laughing. If you lose your focus, go back-to-back again, regain your focus, and try again." It may take a few tries before students are successfully able to complete this first step. Then, at your direction, the students make eye contact with another person and, without talking, switch partners. This activity takes a long time for the group to master, but when it does, a focused silence will take over the room.
- *Blind trust walk*. Ask the students to choose persons A and B. Person A leads person B, who has her eyes closed, around the room. Person A needs to take care of person B, making sure she doesn't bump into anyone and feels completely safe. This activity takes place in complete silence. Model different ways to lead: from behind with hands on shoulders, from the side with a hand on an elbow, or with an arm around a shoulder. During the activity the students may switch from one way of holding the partner to another, almost like a dance. The students then repeat the activity with person B leading. In a variation, rather than leading by touch, the leader may give spoken directions in a quiet voice.
- *Blind trust walk* II. This time the leader may leave the follower at any time. The leader will gently indicate, without talking, perhaps with a pat on the shoulder or a squeeze of the hand, that he is leaving the follower. In silence, the leader finds another follower in the room. The follower remains in place, frozen and still, until another leader comes to pick him up. The follower must always keep his eyes closed, even when a new person begins to lead. Emphasize that the students need to take care of everyone in the class. If someone is left for a long time, it can be disconcerting. The class might reflect on the activity afterward, considering questions like, "What did it feel like to be led by different people you didn't know? To be left the first time? For a long period of time? What happens to your other senses when you lose sight?"
- *Mirroring*. Students face each other. Throughout the activity, students maintain eye contact. ("Stare Down," listed above, is good practice for this.) One person slowly begins to move in place. The other person

follows, mirroring the leader's exact movements. Students will often try to trick each other, moving quickly so their partner can't follow. Encouraging students to move slowly and take care of their partners. As they continue to mirror, ask them to switch leaders fluidly and without stopping. After a few more minutes, ask the students to move leadership back and forth between the two without talking. Finally, ask the students to make eye contact with another person in the room and, without stopping, to begin mirroring the movements of the new person, crossing the space to stand next to that person and continuing to shift leadership.

Forum Theatre

Forum Theatre, created by Augusto Boal, begins with a play script whose plot contains an oppression recognizable to the audience. At the completion of the performance, the production begins again, though in condensed form. At any point in the production, an audience member—Boal calls them spec-actors—calls out "Stop" and takes the place of the actor and changes the course of the performance in order to overthrow the oppression. The other actors continue to perpetuate the oppression. The audience joins the action in one of several possible ways that evaluate the direction the plot is taking, suggest other options, or become spec-actors to change the course of events.

Many variations are possible. Working with August Wilson's *The Piano Lesson*, for example, students may perform a section of the play in which the core conflict is being played out and invite other students to improvise to create an alternative to Wilson's text. This may be a whole-class or small-group activity. It may be presented informally as an activity for one class period or more fully developed into a formal performance.

The Cordel

At its essence, the cordel is remarkably simple, since it only consists of a clothesline and clothespins. And yet these simple materials can be used in a variety of ways to display student work and to delineate a space for performances. When we use the cordel in workshops, we prefer to find a space separate from the workshop area. We might hang the clothesline between two trees in the garden outside the school or between two walls in the school's entrance. Students then know their work will be made public at the end of the experience.

In this chapter we told the story of an epic cordel that circled an entire lake. As dramatic as this example is, this is not typical of the ways cordels might become a part of the learning environment. At Habla: The Center for Language and Culture in Merida, Mexico, teachers have installed two permanent cordels in classrooms. In one classroom—a space for elementary students—they hung two pieces of painted wood on opposite sides of a wall, floor to ceiling. They attached a string to one side of the wood panel at the top of the wall and then brought it across to the other side and attached it. They then returned the string to the first side but a little lower, again attaching it to the panel. Continuing, they formed a zigzag pattern of string down the wall so that work might be hung at every level from the floor to the ceiling. In a classroom for older students, Mark Durgee used the cordel as a way of sharing and displaying ongoing student work. He wanted the cordel to be invisible, so instead of clothesline or string he used fishing line. He, too, formed a zigzag pattern on the wall. Throughout the semester, his students took black-and-white photographic self-portraits and wrote poetry and stories. The wall became a beautiful gallery of work that evolved as the class progressed.

Daniel Soares uses the cordel as a way of having the students in his school in Brazil share work among various classes. His cordel is permanently installed in the school's hallway, and students post work from their classrooms as a way of building a learning community *across* classrooms.

In all of these examples, it's important that the work displayed on a cordel is of a quality and nature that an audience is compelled to experience it. It's best not to use the cordel to hang up a problem set in mathematics or a set of vocabulary quizzes. The cordel is most effective when meaningful work is shared among the students and with a wider audience.

The overall aesthetic of the cordel needs to be considered as the assignment is created. One way to do this is to develop a guiding concept for the cordel, such as *stories from childhood* or *imaginary worlds*. It's also useful to carefully consider what materials will be used to create the work that will be displayed. Students in Mark Durgee's class took only black-and-white photographs and displayed writing using black or white markers and pencils. Similarly, Kurt Wootton gave his students twelve-inch squares of craft paper as a foundation and then black paper to create images that would be pasted onto craft paper. On one side of the craft paper they created a black silhouette of an image of a story they wrote. On the other side they wrote a story, so the cordel could be viewed from both sides. Limiting the color palate and the materials—and choosing a guiding concept—makes the cordel a compelling installation rather than just a random collection of student work.

3

Entering Text

Exploring Possible Worlds

The Breeze at dawn has secrets to tell you
Don't go back to sleep.
You must ask for what you really want.
Don't go back to sleep
People are going back and forth across the doorsill
Where the two worlds touch.
The door is round and open
Don't go back to sleep.

—Rumi

All art enables acting as if. But such acting always moves toward something . . .
Art always pushes toward some sense of connection and completion.

—Shirley Brice Heath

ONE MORNING IN LATE JANUARY, in the bustling, brightly lit library of Central High School in St. Paul, Minnesota, thirty people—students, teachers, and artists—stand in a circle in the center of the open space. The group is meeting to design a curriculum for an Introduction to English course for ninth graders at Central High School. Two aspects of this gathering are unique: the Performance Cycle provides the curriculum design model, and equal numbers of teachers, visiting artists, and high school students compose the planning team.

The initial unit will be based on August Wilson's *The Piano Lesson*, a play soon to open at St. Paul's highly regarded Penumbra Theater. In addition to reading, reflecting on, and responding to a print version of the play, all the students and their families will be invited to attend a performance at Penumbra. In today's initial meeting, veteran theater teacher Jan Mandell will introduce the planning group to the Performance Cycle. Later, she will ask them to develop a compelling focus question and set of activities that ninth graders will find relevant and interesting.

As their work begins, soft music plays in the background, and Jan says quietly, "Let's focus our attention and begin." She makes a small graceful movement with her forearms, opening them out in welcome, then bringing them together at her midsection. Everyone repeats the gesture. The combination of music, quiet voice, and gentle movements are immediately calming.

At her direction, everyone begins to move slowly around the room in a series of initial community-building activities (see "For the Classroom"). She continues, "As you walk, make eye contact. When I give the signal, stop and greet the person in front of you with your eyes. Acknowledge the presence of others in the room."

Soon, pairs are leading one another silently through a mirroring exercise, one partner reflecting the gestures of the other. The music continues.

After a moment, Jan says, "We recognize the presence and value of everyone in the room. Later we'll introduce ourselves to the work of authors who decided that the people they write about have so much value that they took a long time, many years, to put them into books. August Wilson gave us an entire century of African American life. Even though he's gone, that story and these truths remain for all of us to learn, just as your stories will remain when you are gone."

The mirror-making continues until Jan speaks again, "Now silently thank your partner and continue to walk. Notice that as a teacher you don't need any special experience to teach in this way. You can come right into this. You've got everything you need when you enter a classroom." She continues, "Find another person, stop and stand face to face." She pauses while new pairs form. "Talk to your partner. Tell him why you've come to this work."

With these directions, the atmosphere becomes sociable and chatty. People exchange names, hold brief conversations, then move on. Later, at Jan's direction, everyone has gathered into a large circle. Each participant offers his or her name along with an identifying gesture. The group then responds in unison, repeating the name and gesture.

Next, the group transitions to a technique called sculpting.[1] In these exercises, one person acts as sculptor. Using another person as his clay, the sculptor creates a statue that represents a specific idea or emotion. In a few short moments, the room fills with living sculptures in a variety of poses. Following Jan's directions, the group creates a "museum of living, breathing, feeling moments." She then teaches them to create tableaus in which two or more statues combine to form images of themes and characters drawn from *The Piano Lesson*.

> Even before we begin working with a text, we take it off the page. We bring the characters to life so we can see and feel what's going on. By teaching in this way, you are not only teaching to the mind, but to the heart and to the emotions, which is really why these authors write.

These exercises—the Human Atom, Mirroring, the Name Game, Sculpting, Tableaus—establish the foundation for a classroom community. In this brief time, Jan has demonstrated that the work to come will be active and serious; it will be purposeful, social, and relatively risk-free.

They will be directed precisely and with confidence. Though some activities may be unfamiliar, nothing will be beyond their ability or too challenging to undertake. They are in competent hands.

Set in Pittsburgh in the 1930s, *The Piano Lesson* centers on a conflict between Berniece and Boy Willie, siblings who have inherited a piano. Their great-grandfather, a former slave, had carved their family's history on the piano and Berniece and Boy Willie must now decide whether to keep the piano, as Berniece wishes, or sell it so that Boy Willie can use his half to buy land.

To begin the work, Jan asks the "sculptors" to think about a family conflict.

> Often in family conflict, both sides are right. In many August Wilson plays, both sides are right. In *The Piano Lesson*, one person wants to sell the piano, and one person wants to keep the piano. They're both right. And the working out of those kinds of ties and those kinds of conflicts is what we're focused on here. So what I'm going to ask you do is to identify some kind of family conflict you know about. It doesn't have to be profound, and it must be one you are willing to share. Go inside yourself. Try to get beyond the "do the dishes, don't do the dishes" kind of conflict. One person in the group sculpts the other three. Do it without talking.

As the background music plays, three-person sculptures appear around the room, carefully positioned in a striking arrangement of shapes. Once the tableaus are set, Jan reconvenes the group, and one by one trios showcase their work. In one set of figures, a young person pulls away from a group that is reaching out to her. Another represents a family huddled together protectively. "This is my family inheritance," the student explains in describing the close-knit group.

Jan takes note of the word *inheritance*. As the planning workshops continue, that word is repeated often. Eventually it provides the language for the question each class will use as the unit's centerpiece: "What will I do with the inheritance I have received?" By beginning with community-building activities and then exploring the major themes from a core text, the group arrives at a student-focused essential question that will guide the unit. The question is personal, direct and clear enough to engage students. It provides a way into reading and discussing both the text and the students' lived experiences.

In addressing this question, students will need to consider many facets of inheritance. What is the inheritance they themselves have received? From what sources? And finally, what will they make with what they have been given? By the end of the first day, the planning group's work has a name: the Inheritance Project. Now the task is to design a curriculum and series of activities so that ninth grade classrooms become interesting, lively, and productive sites for teaching and learning.

INTRODUCING TEXT: *THE PIANO LESSON*

Actor James Williams steps into the center of the circle. "Let me tell you about *The Piano Lesson*," he says.

A St. Paul resident and long-time friend of August Wilson, Williams was a member of the original Broadway cast of *The Piano Lesson*. In a deep, resonant actor's voice, he begins to talk about August Wilson's life and his plays, connecting them to the family conflict tableaus he watched the groups construct.

"I'm going to read a section from the play. Then you can talk about how it connects to your life. Later, you can read and talk about the whole play." He pauses. "Now I'm going to let Mr. Wilson talk."

Williams reads a monologue from the play. Performing Uncle Doaker's lines, he recounts how the piano was traded back and forth by two white plantation owners. The reading ends: "Sutter ain't had no money. But he had some niggers. So he asked . . . if maybe he could trade off some of his niggers for that piano. Told him he would give him one and half niggers for it. That's the way he told him. Say he could have one full grown and one half grown."[2] Williams puts down the book and looks up at the group gathered around him. The room is silent.

Corey, a high school senior, speaks up. "I've got to learn to read like that. It was awesome."

Another student adds, "It wasn't like you were reading it. It was like you are that person."

The conversation turns to the plot of the play and finally to its language. "Mr. Wilson says it so casually," Williams points out. "'They traded some niggers to get the piano.' That is so intense."

Once broached, the topic of the n-word becomes the focus of the conversation. Many in the room want to talk about the ways they hear the word used in everyday conversation in school hallways and classrooms, in their neighborhoods, and in the media. People speak energetically and listen attentively. Finally, the talk turns back to the word's use in *The Piano Lesson*. The group decides that in teaching *The Piano Lesson*, classroom teachers will have to address the use of the word directly. Teacher Cornelius Rish, whose background is teaching social studies and drama, volunteers to visit classrooms and lead discussions.

Jan summarizes:

> We have to deal with the language of the play. We have to have these conversations. They force us to be uncomfortable and to face what we have inherited. Nobody knows the right way to talk about this. We've all inherited a history of racism. We didn't make it. But if we don't deal with it, we will continue to make more history for our children to inherit. Let's figure it out now. It's a great teaching moment.

With this very first encounter with the text, the group embarks on what will be a challenging but deeply rewarding exploration of Wilson's world. As they engage further, they will address issues that are personally relevant, discuss the language of the text, study the contents and structure of the play, and embody their work in a performance that synthesizes the most important aspects of what they have learned.

ENTERING TEXT: EXPLORING THE LANDSCAPE

Some young people come to school believing journeys into literature are important, interesting, and well within their capacity to understand and make use of. Others, for a variety of reasons—often well justified—believe otherwise. What encourages students, in the words of the poet Rumi, to join "the people going back and forth across the doorsill / where the two worlds touch" and to explore humanity's written record?[3]

In his classic study of schools, educator John Goodlad described classrooms as characteristically having a flat affect, a climate that promotes disengagement and boredom.[4] Following Goodlad, Ornstein and Levine highlighted five basic patterns in typical classroom culture:

- The classroom is generally organized as a group that the teacher treats as a whole. This pattern seems to arise from the need to maintain "orderly relationships" among twenty to thirty people in a small space.
- "Enthusiasm and joy and anger are kept under control." As a result, the general emotional tone is "flat" or "neutral."
- Most student work involves "listening to teachers, writing answers to questions, and taking tests and quizzes." Textbooks and workbooks generally constitute the "media of instruction."
- These patterns become increasingly rigid and predominant as students proceed through the grades.
- Instruction seldom goes beyond "mere possession of information." Little effort is made to arouse students' curiosity or to emphasize thinking.[5]

These types of classrooms do little to encourage students to connect with or pay attention to course content. Seated at their desks, expected to be motionless and silent, students often engage in what we call *minimal monitoring*. They devote just enough attention to the progress of the class to save themselves from being embarrassed if called on. If, for example, the class is taking turns reading aloud, students will pay just enough attention to pick up smoothly where the previous reader stopped. As long as they are monitoring at a basic level, many focus most of their attention elsewhere—on the activities of their peers, the view out the classroom window, or the world inside their own heads. If they are sufficiently skilled, they can even use the time to complete homework for another class or send text messages.

Teachers and artists like Jan Mandell create an entirely different classroom environment. Using the full range of tools at their disposal, they raise questions, tell stories, awaken curiosity, and provide a pathway for exploration. They lead the way, charting the path, infusing energy, and offering encouragement. They call for students' undivided attention. In the same spirit, eminent arts educator Maxine Greene describes the imagination as "the felt possibility of looking beyond the boundary where the backyard ends or the road narrows . . . These paths are promises about where we might reach if we tried."[6] Greene sees imaginative learning as a limitless process. Once students begin to work in this way, a class can engage deeply with course material in a shared exploration of the landscape they have created.

Nonetheless, the first few steps across the doorsill as they "enter the text" may prove difficult for students accustomed to minimal monitoring as a classroom norm. The initial moments when they are asked to leave their seats and stand before their classmates may be especially intimidating. Adolescents who are grappling with identity issues and sensitive to the judgment of peers may fear becoming visible and vulnerable. Adults may fear losing control of the group, or may themselves not be comfortable with the participation required.

Yet, as Greene explains, once students overcome fear and inertia, these moments are rich with possibility. The working environment feels transformed, energized, filled with potential. Once shared and exchanged, positive energy increases exponentially, creating a reserve for all to draw on and a palpable sense of solidarity and support. By establishing a landscape of focused energy and rewarded risk, the classroom becomes an interesting, lively, and productive canvas for teaching and learning.

In precisely this spirit, Entering Text activities are carefully structured to raise questions, introduce language, and inspire exploration through visualization, improvisation, embodiment, repetition, and discussion. Entering Text activities help students develop receptive minds, widen their learning horizons, and discover new terrain.

EMBODYING AND IMPROVISING

A growing body of literature suggests that physical activity plays a significant part in developing cognitive capacity. Challenging the age-old dichotomy between mind and body, neuroscientists, linguists, and philosophers now accept that mimetic activities—movement and gesture—function as fundamental aspects of human intelligence and that moving and thinking are not, as Descartes proposed, separate phenomenon.[7] Instead, these processes support and inform one another, providing essential information for both performers and observers.

In planning an ArtsLiteracy workshop to introduce the landmark memoir *The Autobiography of Frederick Douglass: An American Slave, Written by Himself,* held just a month after Barack Obama's election to the presidency in 2008, Jan and Eileen asked participants to compare the Douglass and Obama biographies.[8] They handed out written summaries of both men's lives, then divided them into episodes to be performed as tableaus. An example of a brief written summary read, "Douglass was taken from his mother when he was still an infant. He then lived with his grandmother, Betty Bailey, but was taken from her at age six." Workshop participants then divided into groups and created a tableau of their assigned section of both biographies.

Soon the participants assembled and presented a performance. Actor James Williams began by reading excerpts from Obama's speech on race.[9] Then, one by one, groups read and performed their tableaus for the entire workshop. Finally, everyone received and read a one-page biography of each man. In this way, the presenters performed both Douglass's and Obama's stories. As one teacher-observer later noted, "My method of introducing students to an author's biography has been to create a handout and read it aloud to students in class. The performance approach is vastly more powerful." This approach proved lively, participatory, engaging, and memorable. The activity brought the material to life and invited what researchers call *embodied cognition*, the idea that cognitive processes lie deeply rooted in the body's interactions.

Kinesthetic activities such as the tableau support learning in a variety of ways. Motor experiences influence memory and problem-solving abilities. As students enact events, beliefs, feelings, and ideas, these experiences become and remain memorable, in part because performances incorporate the *paralinguistic* features of language: tone of voice, facial expression, gesture, posture. The work of Susan Goldin-Meadow demonstrates that children given math problems ordinarily considered too difficult for them have increased success when encouraged to gesture while thinking.[10] Work of this sort suggests that actions appear to bypass the conscious reasoning brain altogether to aid people in arriving at solutions.

> Telling children to gesture encourages them to convey previously unexpressed, implicit ideas, which in turn makes them receptive to instruction that leads to learning. Gesturing appears to help children to produce new problem-solving strategies, which in turn gets them ready to learn. The findings extend previous research that body movement not only helps people to express things they may not be able to verbally articulate, but actually to think better.[11]

When learning embodies kinesthetic work, not only performers but also spectators benefit. When a person watches a performance, language and paralinguistic features combine to heighten attention, command more attentional capacity, and activate mirror neurons in the brain. These neurons "respond when we see someone else performing an action—or even when we hear an action described—as if we ourselves were performing the action. By simultaneously playing a role in both acting and thinking, mirror neurons suggested that the two might not be so separate after all."[12]

For students who struggle to access the rich layers of meaning embedded in written language, performance work uses their expertise with spoken language, building the logical, semantic, and grammatical skills crucial to advanced literacy. By making content available to be discussed, and refined, performance work amplifies the collective knowledge of the classroom community and broadens learning opportunities for students.

NURTURING RECEPTIVE LEARNERS

Some students easily derive meaning from print. Others struggle to decode. Students' positions on the literacy continuum may be largely unrelated to their interest in concepts and ideas. Entering Text activities introduce topics and questions through media such as visual art, music, dance, puppetry, film, and theater and through brief, evocative portions of print texts. These multimodalities aim to improve fluency, word knowledge, and comprehension so that students may develop the focus, stamina, and effort to explore the core text further and to think more deeply about the topic at hand.

"Sharing images at the beginning, when students may not know how to articulate what they think or how they feel encourages discussion that focuses on description rather than judgment."[13] An exploratory or provisional discussion presents a wide range of options to investigate as participants move further into a text. Images offer the groundwork for making predictions that group members can refer to as the work continues.

Receptive learners demonstrate dispositions to learn. These dispositions include becoming alert to opportunities to learn and the inclination to use their developing skills.[14] Entering Text activities support students' dispositions to learn by bringing words to life, focusing their thoughts and attention, helping them to think imaginatively about the text, and drawing on their many intelligences.

RAISING QUESTIONS

Teaching with questions is an ideal way to encourage students to enter new territory. Questions like, "What will I do with the inheritance I have received?" are invitations to explore and create. These questions differ greatly from the known-answer questions teachers ordinarily ask. They address big ideas and point in two directions: inward to students' own lives and outward to the content of a text. They suggest that students have important contributions to make. They encourage students to do more than minimally monitor classroom activities. When incorporated into the Performance Cycle, questions like these provide a direction for ongoing activities and a focus for the final performance. Some educators call them *Essential Questions* and describe them as:

- "Important questions that recur throughout all our lives." They are "broad in scope and timeless by nature."
- "Core ideas and inquiries within a discipline." They "point to the core of big ideas in a subject and to the frontiers of technical knowledge. They are historically important and alive in the field."
- Helping "students effectively inquire and make sense of important but complicated ideas, knowledge, and know-how—a bridge to findings that experts may believe are settled but learners do not yet grasp or see as valuable."
- Questions that "will most engage a specific and diverse set of learners." They "hook and hold the attention of your students."[15]

When Rick Benjamin, poet, teacher, and social activist, led a workshop at a weekend-long ArtsLiteracy conference for teachers, students, and artists, he began with a series of personal stories about the power of awareness. He talked about looking carefully at ordinary things, like a leaf or snowfall, of thinking carefully about a conversation with a stranger or a moment with children. Into this compelling talk, an invitation to be alert and mindful, he wove a series of poems he recited from memory. He culminated with the Lucille Clifton poem "whose side are you on?"

> the side of the busstop woman
> trying to drag her bag
> up the front steps before the doors
> clang shut i am on her side
> i give her exact change
> and him the old man hanging by
> one strap his work hand folded shut
> as the bus doors i am on his side

> when he needs to leave
> i ring the bell i am on their side
> riding the late bus into the same
> someplace i am on the dark side always
> the side of my daughters
> the side of my tired sons[16]

Rick was silent for a moment to let the force of the poem resonate. Then, one by one, he pointed out the evocative details Clifton uses to draw her reader into the scene. He calls attention to the powerful question "whose side are you on?" and the call-and-response structure of her inventive repetitions: "i am on her side," "his side," "their side," "i am on the dark side always."

After a pause, he asked, "Whose side are you on? Let's write about it. If it works for you, begin your poem with the phrase 'I am on the side of . . .' and take it from there."

With barely any hesitation, everyone wrote. Before the workshop ended, members of the group produced some remarkable poetry and many volunteers read their work aloud.

Later Rick commented: "In a class or workshop, you can't expect writing to come out of thin air. As a teacher, I see my job as creating *thick air*, an environment where we are all inspired to write and, for a moment at least, overcome our fear of failure. We believe that we can. I get things started and everyone takes it from there."

Rick creates an environment that inspires writing. The act of what we've come to call *creating thick air,* of orchestrating occasions when everyone is inspired to create, represents the best work that the best teachers do and has become a guiding principle of our work.

In designing an ArtsLiteracy workshop on teaching *Macbeth*, Jan, Eileen, and Kim Colbert, a St. Paul English teacher, decided to focus on a theme often addressed when *Macbeth* is taught: unbridled ambition. In planning sessions, we discussed possible questions. While the general concept seemed compelling, the term *unbridled ambition* didn't seem quite right: it wasn't the kind of language adolescents use. How could we get the idea across using more age-appropriate language? We considered many questions, including these:

- What happens to make a fundamentally good person become evil?
- How do you identify the boundary between good and evil?
- What truths must you always live by?
- What does it mean to win? What does it mean to lose?

Finally, we settled on the question: "What makes a person cross a line that changes his/her life?" We felt that the metaphor of crossing a line was general and yet tangible enough that students could find examples in their own lives as well as in Shakespeare's tragedy. In the workshop, which included teachers, artists, and students, the question led to a series of rich discussions and performances. We began by asking, "What does it mean to cross a line?" and continued by exploring additional questions: What examples of crossing a line can you think of from your own lives? When did the characters in *Macbeth* cross a line? What were their reasons?

In planning the workshop designed around *The Autobiography of Frederick Douglass* and the Barack Obama speech on race, we titled the unit "From Frederick Douglass to Barack Obama: To Shape Our Future." Introducing the unit, we presented these questions: What do you see in your future? What can you imagine? What will you do to shape your future? In yet another ArtsLiteracy workshop, we organized a study of the Icarus and Daedalus myth in Ovid's *Metamorphoses* around the question, "What would the world be like if people didn't take risks?"

The Piano Lesson workshop led by Jan and Eileen in St. Paul was the first in which students were centrally involved in designing the Essential Question. The question they developed turned out to be one of the most successful. Though initially intended as the basis for a monthlong unit, "What will you do with the inheritance you received?" proved so generative that teachers used it throughout the entire semester, weaving together units on *Romeo and Juliet,* poetry reading and writing, and an introduction to conducting and writing up research.

ENCOUNTERING LANGUAGE

Creating Essential Questions offers a relatively straightforward way to introduce students to challenging texts like *Macbeth*. Helping them negotiate unfamiliar language and style is another matter entirely. In Shakespeare's language, for example, readers encounter unfamiliar words as well as familiar words with unexpected meanings. They come across sentences with unusual word arrangement and words with missing syllables or parts of syllables.[17] Yet, it is not only Shakespeare's Elizabethan tongue that students find daunting. Even the language of modern-day books is often a challenge. The structure and length of sentences, the unfamiliar vocabulary, and the need to construct meaning require proficiencies many adolescents lack. For most students, reading the texts required in secondary school curriculum is not easy.

Approaches that introduce students to small portions of texts at the outset of a unit often help. In teaching *Macbeth*, after reading and discussing a summary of the plot and characters, participants engage in an activity called Tossing Sentences. They receive slips of paper containing a sentence or phrase, such as, "If it were done when 'tis done, then 'twere well it were done quickly" or "Bloody instructions, which, being taught, return to plague the inventor." Working in pairs, they read their text aloud several times and discuss possible meanings. They then create a tableau that represents the meaning of the text, compare their tableau with other groups, and discuss similarities and differences. Finally, they receive copies of the full soliloquy or scene (see "For the Classroom").

These activities especially benefit English language learners. For those not yet fluent with the language, repeated rehearsal and performance with brief, manageable sections of text provide opportunities to practice sound-symbol relationships and to own the reading process. When students make artistic decisions based on their understanding of the text, they develop courage and interest in learning and sharing what they know.

VISITING MANGO STREET

"We didn't always live on Mango Street. Before that we lived on Loomis on the third floor, and before that on Keeler."[18] So begins a book that is assigned to many middle and high school student across America. *The House on Mango Street* is brief, the typeface is large, the narrator is a young Latino, the language is beautifully poetic, and the vocabulary is at the middle school reading level. Organized in brief vignettes, the book lends itself to "bites" suitable for in-class or at-home reading and autobiographical writing. All in all, it's a perfectly teachable book

In truth, *The House on Mango Street* is a deceptively difficult book. Students who do best with a limited and clearly delineated cast of characters and a straightforward plot and time sequence are likely to find its episodic and poetic style, cast of thirty-six characters, shifting time frame, and lack of a linear plot structure highly challenging. In a classroom we observed, one hard-working and capable student wondered out loud why they were reading this book. "I just don't get it. This is so confusing. I'm lost from the very first page. What's the point of this book?"

Unless teachers find ways to make the point of reading clear to students and bring texts to life, students may cover up their disinterest and confusion by using one of their most effective weapons, the phrase that strikes a dagger into the heart of all teachers: "This is *so* boring!" They may turn to Spark Notes just to earn a passing grade or to avoid being hassled. They may write their autobiographical essay about their house or their hair and at the same time never ask: If this episodic, poetic narrative is not about houses or hair, what exactly is it about? What does it have to do with me? Why should I read it?

These are useful big-picture questions. However, most curriculum documents we've encountered offer little help to students as they seek answers to these questions. Instead, they create criteria clarifying what it means to be "college and career ready" and establishing the benchmarks students must demonstrate along the way, presenting these to educators using technical language. The Common Core State Standards for English language arts, for example, establishes ten anchor standards for literature in grades 6–12. These define the skills and understandings that all students must demonstrate, including mastery of (1) key ideas and details; (2) textual craft and structure; (3) knowledge and ideas; and (4) a range of complex literary and informational texts.[19]

While lists of this sort may well represent what mature, committed readers and writers do and establish some uniformity for educators, these lists never seem to take a learner's perspective or establish an appropriate foundation for students' purposes. Instead, they concentrate on knowledge and skills that students often see as having little connection to their lives and worlds. Often educators pass these expectations on to students with little or no intervening explanation. Instead, they naturalize expectations and skip the "why" question. When students begin to see themselves as readers and writers, they may become interested in the mechanics of the craft. Until then, readers are likely to demonstrate their understanding of textual craft and structure only as a means of complying with institutional expectations, though they are very likely to care about taking in or creating a great story, learning how characters solve problems, and applying what they take from texts to the life situations they encounter.

Why do we want students to read *The House on Mango Street?* Or, for that matter, any other work of fiction? Because, first and foremost, we hope that reading will open the world, offer a wide horizon, and suggest journeys—both literal and metaphorical—to places readers may otherwise not go. Reading has the capacity to focus and deepen their thinking, offering new perspectives and insights. How do teachers and artists create an environment that opens new worlds and helps readers gain the tools they need to make sense of those worlds? Before expecting students to engage in high levels of analysis and critique, we must help them focus and make sense of a text and come to understand how it might matter to them.

With these thoughts in mind, Eileen and John Holdridge, an Arts-Literacy staff member and resident artist, designed a workshop on teaching *The House on Mango Street*. In preparing, they did their best to take the perspective of the perplexed student. A careful reading of the very first paragraph suggested reasons for inexperienced readers to be confused. Look at the subtlety, time sequence, and compression in the first four brief sentences: "We didn't always live on Mango Street. Before that we lived on Loomis on the third floor, and before that we lived on Keeler. Before Keeler it was Paulina, and before that I can't remember. But what I remember most is moving a lot."[20] These sentences not only imply that we—whoever we are—presently live on Mango Street, but also they sketch a family's frequent relocations and suggest a pattern that is likely to continue. The remaining three sentences on the page continue what for many students may be a dizzying linguistic ride, alternating twice between present and the past. Then on to the future: the dream house with real stairs and a big yard.

Frequent moves from one crowded apartment to another is an experience many students in urban schools find familiar. Yet, as with so many truly important topics, it is a subject unlikely to be discussed in school. Like many other aspects of Mango Street, the topic of frequent moves and crowded dwellings appears in an impressionistic and oblique way. While this is one of the beautiful qualities of the text, it is also one of its challenges. Eileen and John wanted to make this fast-moving textual kaleidoscope stand still long enough for readers to begin to understand and care about Esperanza's story and to develop questions that will carry them through a full reading of the narrative. They planned to introduce the text in three ways: by enacting representations of Esperanza's several homes, past, present, and the dream future; by creating a living image of Mango Street itself; and by reading and bringing to life selections of the text that describe several key characters who represent possible models for Esperanza's future. These Entering Text activities anchored a chronological reading, discussion, and response to the entire text.

To create visual representations of the three houses, John and Eileen asked students to do a careful study of the first vignette, which moves rapidly among past, present, and future. Always wary of worksheets that can squeeze the life out of even the most captivating book, they nonetheless created a text map of three simple boxes to help students clarify and dramatize the contrast between Esperanza's many houses.

Participants worked in groups of six. After explaining their plan to create a performance that would bring Esperanza's world to life, they asked each group to read and discuss the first vignette and fill in the text map. People shared ideas and asked one another questions. Many questions they asked had to do with temporal cues and differences in tenses, subtleties less skilled readers often miss. "How'd you figure that out?" students asked more than once. "See, it says here . . . ," came the replies. The structure of the workshop encouraged everyone to be open about what they hadn't noticed and others to respond with support and without condescension.

Earlier, during the session warm-up, everyone had learned to create statues, then tableaus (see "For the Classroom"). After completing the text map, each group used its handout to create a series of three snapshot tableaus, each representing Esperanza's house at a different point in time—past, present, and future.

John coached groups in their tableaus, encouraging more and more vivid representations. He then asked them to add a few lines of dialogue, drawing explicitly from the text or created from an idea implied in the text. A final rehearsal prepared them to perform for one another. The results were riveting; words on the page came alive. In the tableaus, bodies came to represent houses, tiny, cramped, crumbling, with broken pipes and boarded-up windows. Two groups performed this exchange between young Esperanza and a nun:

> Once when we were living on Loomis, a nun from my school passed by and saw me playing out front . . .
> "Where do you live?" she asked.
> "There." I said pointing up to the third floor.
> "You live *there*?"[21]

Each group repeated these brief phrases several times, succinctly and vividly. Each time we felt Esperanza's misery and shame. Each time we saw the houses transform and expand into dream houses with stairs and a yard and with room to move and breathe. Finally, as a happy accident, the group that performed last presented a transition back from the dream house of the future to the cramped, crumbling houses of the present and then added these words from the text:

> "For the time being," Mama says.
> "Temporary." says Papa.
> But I know how these things go.[22]

As the presentation ended, the room was totally quiet. It was the kind of silence that punctuates those rare moments in school when a group knows it has made a bit of magic and feels the power of their creation. The students inhabited the world of a text, explored its landscape, and connected it to their own lived experience.

FOR THE CLASSROOM

ENTERING TEXT

The Sculpture Garden

This activity builds on the statue exercises begun during community building. In pairs, students create sculptures of words, images, or themes from the text. One person in each pair is designated the sculptor, the other clay. When you call out a word or phrase, the sculptor molds the clay into its representation. Silence is maintained throughout. Music provides a mood-setting background for this activity. Once sculpted, the clay remains frozen. Once you give a signal, sculptors wander the garden, observing their creations.

Later the sculptor and clay exchange roles and repeat the activity. After students have worked in pairs, two groups join and a sculptor works with three pieces of clay, providing a basic approach to forming tableaus. This activity offers numerous opportunities for reflection on both the process and the product. What aspect of the word or phrase do the various sculptures illustrate? Which images stand out? In what ways are the individual sculptures the same, or different? Another option is to offer sculptors the opportunity to sculpt by gesture rather than touch. If sculptors model by touch, they should do so with respect and care.

Tableau

A tableau is a frozen image of an event, activity, or concept. Groups of four to six students form a tableau that may reflect the vision of a single "sculptor" or a collective creation of the group. Before beginning the activity, offer a simple set of guidelines, suggesting, for example, that everyone in the tableau is physically connected or positioned at different levels in space. Many variations are possible, including creating snapshots—tableaus presented in a series with carefully orchestrated transitions—or tableaus that move or speak.

Again, music played as tableaus are formed and displayed to the group contributes to the activity. When the activity is completed, discussion about both the content and the process increases awareness and understanding.

Rapid Tableaus

Organize the students into small groups. Explain that you will read an image from the text and that the group has until the count of ten to form a tableau without talking. When you reach ten, and they are frozen in their sculptures, tell them to remember where they are in their sculptures. Continue with four more images from the text. Now explain that you will read the five images in quick succession and they will practice moving quickly from tableau to tableau. If they forget where they are, encourage them to improvise in the moment and find a place.

Designate some place in the room as a stage. Then, as someone reads the phrases aloud, have groups perform their tableaus, either singly or two groups at a time. Remind the students that they are on stage in the transitions between the tableaus and need to remain committed throughout the performance.

Tossing/Translating Lines

A number of useful activities combine brief but important segments of text with small group tableaus as a way of entering the text. In the basic Tossing Sentences activity, students receive slips of paper with a line or two from the text they are about to read. They find other people who have the same line and form a tableau that illustrates what they believe to be the meaning of that line. They then create a small performance for others by reading their line aloud while forming their tableau. In preparing the slips beforehand, decide the appropriate size of the tableau groups and distribute the same line to a preselected number of students.

WINDOW SHADE QUOTES

When Theresa Toomey Fox, a Providence, Rhode Island, middle school teacher, introduced her students to Shakepeare's *Othello* in a unit she titled

"Give Me Moor Proof," she posted what she called *window shade quotes* on the blinds in her classroom. In large and readable type, she displayed brief quotations from each of the play's characters. She then asked students to think about what the words revealed about the character and to predict how these key phrases might be important to the play. Iago's words included:

- "I am not what I am" (I.i.65)
- "Trifles light as air / are to the jealous confirmations strong / as proofs of holy writ" (III.iii.322–324)
- "Oh, beware my lord of jealousy / It is the green-eyed monster that doth mock / the meat it feeds on" (III.iii.165–166)
- "Men should be what they seem" (III.iii.127)

Encountering these words every day on the classroom windows, students became familiar with vocabulary, allusions, syntax, and the pace and rhythm of the language. More importantly, though, the words served as clues in a classwide guessing game about who these persons were and what they could figure out about them.

Mapping Texts

Visual maps can help students see the development of many aspects of a text. In St. Paul, teaching artist John Holdridge and Eileen Landay asked the students to read back through the opening vignette of *The House on Mango Street* and write the words and phrases used to describe each of several houses where the narrator had lived. We've also used timelines and maps to explore even more abstract concepts, like the feeling of a book. When elementary students in Mexico read a biography of Frida Kahlo, they created a map of colors that tracked the changing moods and emotions of the narrative.

Character Journeys

Character Journeys give students a glimpse of the arc of a character's development in a play or novel before they actually read the entire story. Place students in groups of three to six. Give each group a line of dialogue from a given character for each person in the group. These lines need to represent the essence of the character's development throughout the story. You might select different characters for each group or the same character for all groups.

Several performance options are possible:

- Each group performs all their lines in any way they would like.
- Each student selects a line, then group members position themselves in the order the lines are spoken. Each student then speaks her line and freezes in a sculpture representing that line. As each person presents her line, we hear and see the arc of the characters' journeys.
- Each person in the group selects a line. The first student creates a sculpture and speaks the line. The second student adds herself to the first person's sculpture and speaks her line. The group continues until a group tableau is formed. Students can then combine tableaus into an entire performance of the character.

The theater group Shakespeare & Company uses this activity as a way of immediately engaging students with Shakespeare's characters and language before beginning to read the play.

Another option is to use Character Journeys as a postreading assessment. Students in small groups review the text and create character journeys for each of the main characters. This activity might be followed by an individual writing assignment where students choose a character and write about that character's journey throughout the text incorporating some of the key selected quotes.

4

Comprehending Text

"Take It, Use It, Make It Your Own"

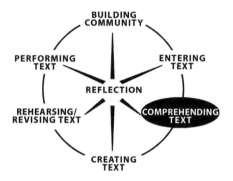

I can't begin to understand this book by sitting alone staring at words on a page.

—CENTRAL HIGH SCHOOL LEADERSHIP TEAM STUDENT

And so they discovered the paradoxical virtue of reading, which is to abstract ourselves from the world in order to make sense of it.

—DANIEL PENNAC, *THE RIGHTS OF THE READER*

IT'S THE MORNING of the second day of the Central High School planning workshop. In small groups, students, teachers, and artists are considering a second text to add to the Inheritance Project curriculum. To do this, they are using a discussion protocol called Final Word. In one group of four, teacher Tyler Scott begins to read aloud a selection from Amy Tan's *The Joy Luck Club.*[1] He has chosen this section because it resonates for him. Before he gives the reason for his choice, he reads the selection aloud, and the other participants offer their thoughts. He explains his reason for choosing the selection and an open discussion follows.

The group sits in a circle and everyone follows along, books in hand, as Tyler reads a description of a Chinese immigrant mother's comical, persistent, and misguided efforts to test her eleven-year-old American-born daughter's potential to be a child prodigy. She checks her daughter's knowledge of obscure facts, asks her to multiply large numbers in her head and to predict the daily temperature in various world capitals. She measures her physical agility by asking her to stand on her head without using her hands. As the young girl tells the story:

> One night I had to look at a page from the Bible for three minutes and then report everything I could remember. "Now Jehoshaphat had riches and honor in abundance and . . . that's all I remember, Ma," I said.
>
> And after seeing my mother's disappointed face once again, something inside of me began to die.[2]

As Tyler reads aloud, the three listeners smile, then laugh. But at the final sentence their smiles fade. After a moment's silence, Ka'Lena, a high school junior, speaks. She begins by describing how her own father compares her unfavorably to her sister and often scolds her for not getting good grades. She continues by recollecting and paraphrasing a passage from another chapter in *The Joy Luck Club* in which another young girl rebels against parental pressure.

Ka'Lena says, "In that part of the story, she told her mother, 'Why do you have to use me to show off?' That line stuck with me because I feel like I can relate to being pushed and prodded and all those things. I feel like I just need to succeed and I just kind of can't."

The other three members of her group listen attentively and nod, her comments resonating. After a moment of silence, Maddy, an actor and teacher, speaks up. "What I really loved about this whole story is this idea of the tension of twos. I see that the chapter is titled, 'Two Kinds' and I noticed the many kinds of twos there are. First, the conflict between the mother and the daughter, the conflict of the two rights. The daughter wants to be her own person and the mother wants her to be some kind of a star. They can only see the wrong in the other one's point of view."

Maddy goes on to point out other instances of what she calls *doubleness* in the story: the doubled point of view of the storyteller, once the rebellious child, now an adult, struggling to understand her own situation and her mother's. She notes that the mother, initially powerful and demanding, is later described as sad and defeated, "blowing away like a small brown leaf, thin, brittle, lifeless." Finally, Maddy contrasts the two different titles in a piano exercise book from her childhood that the storyteller finds after her mother's death. One piece is titled "Pleading Child" and the other "Perfectly Contented."

Sara, another high school student, says, "I want to say something about what the mother is asking her daughter to do." She rereads the section Tyler previously read aloud on identifying capitals, solving math puzzles, reciting a passage from the Bible. "One useless test after another. Kind of like I feel about school." Heads come up from the page and turn toward Sara. Everyone smiles, appreciating the point

Now it's Tyler Scott's turn. He explains that he chose the passage because it reminds him of his relationship with a teenage member of his extended family. "I really was trying to push her academically and I was trying to push her to think about the choices she was making, because you always want to push your kids to be the best they can be and to reach their full potential. But we don't have a rulebook that says, 'Follow this and it will work.'"

"And that's what I thought when I read this story. The mother in the story is from a culture that is very traditional, very disciplined. She tells her daughter, 'You're going to be obedient, and if you do what I tell you to do, hopefully things will work out.' As parents we push, push, push, and push to a point where kids feel they can't be successful. And I look back and I think not about where my cousin went wrong—because I know where she went wrong—but where did I go wrong? And I can't really put my finger on it."

Tyler turns to the students. "How would you like your parents to teach you and challenge you and encourage you to excel and at the same time not pressure you?" It's clear that his is not a known-answer question but a question he asks in order truly to hear the others' perspectives and draw on their expertise.[3]

Ka'Lena responds, "Have you ever heard of the Sandwich Technique? Start with a compliment and then critique and then compliment again." She goes on to give an example of how she wishes her parents would use the Sandwich Technique in their discussions with her, so that rather than be discouraged, as she often is, she will be reassured and encouraged to improve.

There is another moment of silence. Then Scott says simply, "Thank you."

The Final Word discussion protocol is similar to the teaching strategy called Think Aloud, in which a teacher reads a portion of a text aloud to a class and, as the reading continues, stops to question, wonder, and reflect aloud in order to model for students the invisible processes that take place in the minds of proficient readers. Final Word differs from a Think Aloud in several significant ways. First, everyone participates, offering responses to a given passage. Second, the person who chooses and reads the passage offers the final reaction to the selection only after everyone else in the group has commented (see "For the Classroom").

In discussing passages from *The Joy Luck Club*, each person in the group brings a unique perspective to the reading and the conversation, and each takes away a slightly enlarged worldview. Only after everyone has shared very different thoughts does the conversation open to response and discussion. In the process, all members of the group choose and read a selection aloud. They may offer interpretations of the story, explore its themes as well as the writer's style and craft, or tell personal stories. They share something of their own lives and acknowledge the contributions of others. Finally, they may respond to one another with questions, comments, and advice. Everyone teaches and everyone learns. All are engaged in a rich discussion focused on comprehending *The Joy Luck Club*.

WHAT DOES IT MEAN TO COMPREHEND?

Struggling readers is a term educators often use to describe the large numbers of adolescents who cannot read extended academic texts. While the word *struggle* does call attention to the active nature of reading, the term lacks accuracy. It would be more correct to say that many of these students have abandoned the struggle to make meaning from school-related reading. Some, mystified by both purpose and process, refuse to read rather than experience the stigma of being labeled a poor reader. Others reject the demands on their time and attention that reading entails. Still others find the content and style of course material irrelevant and have stopped trying to comprehend it. To help students become proficient readers, educators need to understand what it means to comprehend from the students' perspectives as well as what motivates students to aim for comprehension by embracing the struggles they face in making meaning from text.

The word *comprehension* carries so many shades of meaning that the committee that recently revised Benjamin Bloom's famous taxonomy of educational objectives breaks the word into six categories: remembering, understanding, applying, analyzing, evaluating, and creating.[4] Comprehension encompasses everything from remembering to creating. *The Oxford English Dictionary* stresses the active nature of comprehension, explaining that the word derives from the Latin *comprehendere*, meaning "to seize, grasp, lay hold of, or catch."[5] Seizing requires purpose, attention, focus, and effort. From this point of view, the act of comprehending requires an energetic reach.

In recent years, teachers have taken to teaching comprehension strategies to make the comprehension process visible in classrooms. Often these practices take the form of think-alouds that illustrate a skilled reader's cognitive moves, graphic organizers to help students develop their vocabulary or sort and classify ideas, or structured methods for summarizing key ideas or comparing data from multiple sources. These may be useful steps in helping students practice reading and understanding, especially with complex and challenging texts.[6] However, activities of this sort typically do not address the text's relevance or provide reasons for student engagement. Intended to add clarity, they may instead add an additional layer of obfuscation to what the students are being asked to do.

Educators need a dual perspective: one that understands what it means to be a proficient reader and another that considers what motivates readers to seize the knowledge they gain through extended work with print text. The skillful teacher builds bridges between learner and content and needs to understand both. Many excellent books and journal articles describe comprehension strategies from the teacher's perspective, focusing mainly on how to present, carry out, and evaluate comprehension activities.[7] Fewer explore the question from the students' point of view. In looking for a definition of comprehension, we therefore focus on what makes students grasp content with an energetic reach. To do this, we turned toward the students themselves.

COMPREHENSION: THE LEARNER'S PERSPECTIVE

In February 2008, six St. Paul teachers launched the Inheritance Project in their ninth grade Introduction to English classes. With the help of visiting and resident artists and older high school students, teachers and ninth graders explored the question, "What will I do with the inheritance I have received?" using as the core text August Wilson's *The Piano Lesson* and, as an ancillary text, *The Joy Luck Club*. Through reading, writing, discussing, and participating in an array of performance activities, teachers created curriculum, sharing and revising their plans as they went along. Originally intended to be six weeks long, the unit proved so generative that many teachers extended it throughout the spring semester. They incorporated other texts and additional activities, such as writing and performing poetry and creating and sharing essays in which students researched and wrote about their own inheritance.

Some of the students in the January planning workshop at St. Paul's Central High School were members of Jan Mandell's Leadership Team. These upper-grade students worked with Jan in her acting classes and in the Central Touring Theatre, a group that writes and presents original plays on current social issues relevant to youth. Following the January workshop, some students also became assistants to teachers and mentors to students in ninth grade Inheritance Project classrooms.

In March, Eileen and Maggie Blake, a Brown graduate student, met with the Leadership Team. In a series of e-mail exchanges following their visit, Khymyle Mims a, student leader, discussed his experience as a mentor in Kathryn Johrdahl's ninth grade Introduction to English classroom. Explaining comprehension, Khymyle said, "Comprehension to me is fully understanding something. Whether it be words or numbers or a concept . . . I think to comprehend something is to *take it and use it and make it your own.*"[8]

With Khymyle's permission, we have adopted these categories. In the sections that follow, we enumerate and analyze ways to support students in taking material and ideas, using them, and making them their own.

Comprehension: "Take It"

Establishing environments in which students openly, willingly, and even eagerly focus attention and make the effort to grasp content is an essential first step in laying the groundwork for comprehension. This can be the most challenging step to classroom learning. It is the area in which teachers express the most frustration. "They're just not motivated" is a complaint teachers make about individual students and whole classes. And "lack of motivation" is one way to describe students who appear apathetic, disengaged, or downright resistant. The problem, though, is that by defining the issue in these terms, we place responsibility without seeking a solution. End of story. Yet all of us have seen that motivation varies with circumstances, in part because learning is a social as well as a cognitive act, and motivation is an attribute of groups as well as individuals.

So, how do we create circumstances that invite and encourage students to reach out, to grasp and seize? Place students in an engaged and encouraging group; establish a compelling question or meaningful task; make the audience and purpose for the work clear and specific; and promise students adequate support. Each of these approaches encourages students to want to *take* what educators have to offer.

When the Inheritance Project began in early February, teachers, artists, and student assistants asked their classes to consider the topic of *inheritance*. As they read August Wilson's play, they considered what they had inherited from their ancestors and/or the people who had reared them. In a four-day residency with photographer Usry Alleyne, students created, studied, and discussed photographic self-portraits. They saw that physical characteristics such as the color of hair, eyes, and skin and the shape of faces and noses constituted part of their inheritance. The portraits made that clear. But what else? What about the intangibles, such as mood or disposition? What about customs and traditions? Family history? Teachers knew that for a variety of reasons the topic had the potential to be sensitive and were careful to offer students a wide range of ways to think about the influences in their lives. Through the entire unit, students, teachers and artists created and discussed lists of material objects and, later, personal qualities, traits, interests, and beliefs they had inherited.

For some students, these exercises opened their eyes and gave them an opportunity to explore, discuss, and write about their personal histories and relationships and little-known aspects of their backgrounds and then tie their learning back to key themes in the text. Central High School teachers recognized that the unit interested students. As one teacher said, "Students knew that a number of classes were working on the same project, this inheritance idea, and doing a number of unusual things. I heard them talking about it in the halls between classes. It created something of a buzz in the school."

Early in February all students in the ninth grade Introduction to English classes and their families were invited to attend an evening performance of the Penumbra Theatre's production of *The Piano Lesson*. More than one hundred ninth graders saw the play. Many had never seen a live theater performance before. Actor James Williams visited classes. Repeating the presentation he gave at the planning workshop described in the previous chapter, Williams read Doaker's monologue from *The Piano Lesson* and discussed Wilson's life and work. Students in Cornelius Rish's acting classes created original scenes based on the topic of inheritance. The ninth graders visited the high school's theater classroom to see and discuss the scenes.

Inevitably, there was talk about language. The word *nigger* appears throughout *The Piano Lesson*. Students pointed out that the word is regularly heard in school hallways both as an insult and a term of friendship. Cornelius Rish, who is both a theater and a social studies teacher, visited classes to facilitate discussion on language as an aspect of inheritance. As Rish later described it,

> We talked about the n-word and how it is used, both in hip-hop and in everyday conversation. I wanted students to have an understanding of where the word originated and how it evolved, so I began with the idea of race and asked them where the idea of race came from. Why do we have different racial classifications? We talked about the word *negro* and its original meaning, the color black and how labels developed based on physical characteristics. We talked about how the n-word was used in the past and how today. Students pointed out the distinction many of them made between *nigga* and *nigger*. We talked about their sense that it's okay for people of color to use the word and not okay for white people to use it and how that creates confusion. The students were on all sides of that discussion. No heads were down on desks.[9]

The ninth grade students linked their own experiences and ideas to concepts in Wilson's play and created and presented original performances in their classes. These arts activities and discussions truly helped students *take* from print texts. In her pioneering book *Ways with Words*, anthropologist Shirley Brice Heath uses language virtually identical to Khymyle's. She describes ways of *taking* from books: "As much a part of learned behavior as are ways of eating, sitting, playing games, and building houses." She also suggests that "the ways of taking employed in the school may . . . require substantial adaptation on the part of the child, or may even run directly counter to aspects of the community's pattern."[10]

In the years since Heath first described student literacy learning patterns at home and school, the circumstances have grown even more complex. Many more students in Central's ninth grade classes are English language learners. As native speakers of languages other than English, these students need to develop proficiency in the English language and at the same time learn academic content. Since many come from vigorous, robust oral language and artistic traditions, performance work represents one way they can see their diverse backgrounds not as deficits but as rich funds of knowledge and use them as opportunities to learn.

In addition to a substantial change in student demographics, a second recent shift has changed the type and structure of the texts themselves. Literacy practices in the wider world are very much in transition. The norm in print text has shifted from the page to the screen.[11] Print and visual art now combine in new and ever-changing arrangements and blends. The full palette of information and skills available for students to seize and comprehend increases exponentially. Students regularly text, game, create audio and video, chat, blog, and design Web sites, often simultaneously. Many prove more proficient than their teachers in the use of these tools.

A summary of research on the relationship between media and learning suggests that students develop increased visual-spatial intelligence as a result of using new media in informal learning environments.[12] They understand icons and pictures more quickly and clearly and are able to process and manipulate visual data more effectively. These skills, however, come at the cost of "reflection, analysis, critical thinking, mindfulness, and imagination," attributes essential for academic success.[13] Extended reading of books—both fiction and nonfiction—is decreasing in society at large and especially among teens and young adults. Fifteen-to-twenty-year-olds now spend only seven to ten minutes per day on voluntary reading, about 60 percent less time than the average American.[14] Yet, passage through gateways such as high school graduation and college admissions is still determined by students' demonstrations of their abilities to respond to and create print texts.[15]

By the time unskilled readers enter high school, they are seriously academically disadvantaged. Many have learned to conceal their lack of reading fluency, having learned instead to "read" the classroom conversation well enough to follow the content of the curriculum. In the Inheritance Project classrooms, activities were designed to help students grow as readers, incorporating a wider range of symbol systems, art forms, and learning modalities and linking them directly to practice with print texts.

Central High School English teachers talked with students about how effectively they were managing reading assignments given for homework, using terms like *focus* and *stamina*. They helped them establish schedules for completing assignments, invited adults and older students into their classes as collaborators to model and support young readers, and developed assignments that encouraged students to create performances for real audiences and real purposes, incorporating video, audio, and print. Describing the original scenes his acting class created based on the theme of inheritance, Cornelius Rish explained:

> Each group created a series of narrated connected tableaus. One presented a family's deep religious beliefs. Another showed a family overcoming poverty as a unified group. When the ninth graders came to see the performances, we talked first about family inheritance. They saw the pieces then we had a discussion about what they saw.[16]

The Inheritance Project encouraged students to go far beyond understanding plot, setting, characters, theme, vocabulary, and literary devices or answering end-of-chapter questions. Instead, the emphasis was on creating robust connections between the text and recognizable, important, real-world issues. In describing his work in Kathryn Jordahl's classroom, Khymyle wrote:

> With The Inheritance Project I honestly saw students grasping the meaning [of the word *inheritance*]. When we first began the original reaction was *materialistic*. But after going through activities and deeply discussing

the book we all came to realize that inheritance is deeper. The students and I saw inheritance as both a good and bad thing. They came to understand the basic definition, 'something that is handed or passed down.' It could be AIDS/HIV, study habits, facial expressions, attitudes and moods, eye color or hobbies. We learned that everything you inherit does not have to come from a relative.[17]

For students who have yet to experience the relevance of reading and writing academic texts, comprehension and performance work built around a theme helps them assign meaning to material and to recognize what we have come to call *the authority of text*. Students use skills they may already possess as a scaffold on which to build logical, semantic, and grammatical skills that are crucial to advanced literacy. At the same time, they draw insights from the themes and contents of the work that they can use to negotiate and shape their own personal worlds.

Teachers, too, described students work in the Inheritance Project as differing from the more standard assignments they are asked to complete. Clara Hutchinson described the difference this way:

> For many students, school assignments have very little connection with their lives and no purpose except to pass tests, get through high school, and maybe to aim for college. Even when I hear these students talk about college, I have to wonder how real it is to them. Yet these students are at an age when deep down nothing matters more than purpose. They want to believe their lives have meaning and they can make a difference.[18]

Taking it means not just reading the text at a surface level to pass a test or complete a series of comprehension questions. *Taking it* means connecting with the ideas in a text and considering how they resonate with our lives. We wrestle with the struggles that face the characters; we enter the imaginative world of the author; we move across cultures, borders, and time to engage with other persons' worldviews; we take in informational texts and as a result begin to see our world more fully and vividly.

Comprehension: "Use It"

In many classrooms, the flow of content-related information goes only one way: from teacher to student. Without really understanding how people process information, teachers may conduct their classes as though a pipeline or conduit extends directly from the words they speak into students' ears.[19] This "mug and jug" approach to instruction assumes teachers can pour information directly into students' minds. There is a certain logic to this way of thinking; teachers probably do know more about their subject than students, and they do have reason to move quickly and efficiently to address material they want students to learn. If, however, we want students to seize ideas in the full sense of what it means to comprehend, then we will need to create opportunities for them to do exactly that: to grasp the purpose of what we are teaching, to apply the ideas, and to practice using them.

As the Inheritance Project progressed, teacher Matt Shipman asked his students how they felt about incorporating performance activities into classroom activities. One student replied, "You can actually pretty much live what this person is living. You get to do it yourself and entertain your classmates and it's fun for you. It's like a normal thing you do outside of school. You use your body language and everything."[20] Students often describe how hard it is for them to sit still and listen all through the school day. They are emphatic about the pleasure and value of being able to move around and talk with their peers. When they are able to use performance to "live what [a] person is living" and share what they are learning with their classmates, the experience becomes both meaningful and memorable.

As Ka'Lena, the student who offered the idea of the Sandwich Technique in *The Joy Luck Club* discussion, explained, "It is really hard for me to sit still for a long time. I turn off after a certain time and then can't really be there for a lesson. That numbs my mind. I can't help it; I associate some classes with numbing my mind." Students described the value and pleasure of discussing, improvising, and performing as a way of focusing their attention, watching and listening to others, and physically enacting an idea or event. One student put it simply and plaintively: "Don't teachers know that kids need to move around?"

Activities that involve gesture or mimesis are time-honored methods of exploring meaning. Merlin Donald, a psychologist and cognitive neuroscientist, points out that the human ability to think symbolically is grounded in "mimetic culture" as expressed in traditions like rituals, dance, and craft.[21] Gesture or mimesis provides the basis for comprehending. Opportunities to perform, draw, dance, and sing their understanding of the world and of specific texts enhance students' language and literacy learning.

Modern neuroscience explores this relationship as well. The new field of embodied cognition explores the mind-body connection and studies the role physical activity plays in the development of cognitive capacity. Andy Clark, a philosopher and cognitive neuroscientist, calls the mind a "leaky organ." He describes intelligence and learning as a delicate interplay of brain, body, artifacts, and environment and explains that we think using "action loops that criss-cross the organism and its environment." We learn about the world by performing actions and taking note of the outcomes, the results of which feed into cognition. Thus, perception, movement, and thought are closely bound. As a simple example, Clark uses the act of assembling a jigsaw puzzle, which involves making rough mental determinations, altering the aspect of pieces, looking again, and trying for a fit. This is not a purely mental event: "Completing a jigsaw puzzle thus involves an intricate and iterated dance in which 'pure thought' leads to actions which in turn change or simplify the problems confronting 'pure thought.'"[22]

Performance activities make ideas visible. In Inheritance Project classes, teachers established a pattern of activities that included repeated readings, improvisation, writing, and discussion. Repetition gave students a way to hear and practice the language of the text; improvisation made interpretations visible; writing and discussions provided explicitness, depth, and personal connection. Students rehearsed and presented readings from *The Piano Lesson* and other texts using a full range of approaches, including silent reading, pair-shares, small group, choral, and whole-class activities (see "For the Classroom"). Teachers avoided the usual practice of round robin reading in which students take turns reading unfamiliar text aloud to the whole class. This common classroom practice encourages inattention and passivity while appearing to "cover" the material. A student may read her sentence or paragraph and then turn her attention elsewhere. If she reads aloud poorly, she may anxiously count ahead to figure out what section she will be called on to read in order to practice to avoid humiliation. The meaning of the material may be entirely lost on her.

Unless students are very skilled or invested, taking turns doing cold readings aloud for an entire classroom is rarely a good idea. Instead, students should have the opportunity to invest seriously in using a text by preparing and presenting it to others. In Anthony Jacob's class, for example, students worked in pairs and rehearsed sections of the text and presented fluent, high-quality readings to their peers. Repeated readings of the same section of text using a variety of approaches help students develop reading fluency and vocabulary as well as thoroughly explore meaning.

Improvisations in classrooms also bring words to life, lifting language off the one-dimensional page and reinvesting it with the three-dimensional features of voice, movement, gesture, and timing that are present in every human conversation. In addition, they provide teachers with a significant diagnostic tool for understanding students' minds. When students make their thinking visible through improvisation and performance work, actors/teachers can perceive strengths in and roadblocks to their students' literacy development. When actors and teachers themselves read, improvise, and perform, they model literate behaviors and show their students the mental processes of a proficient reader and thinker. Improvisation also allows students to see the thinking of their peers. Centered on classroom collaboration, performance work gives students a multitude of opportunities to work together and witness how their peers enter and process difficult texts.

Kathryn Jordahl's students worked in groups to explore and develop narratives of their own inheritance. Using photographic self-portraits, music, video, and print, they created original scripts. In March, they opened their classrooms to groups of visiting teachers and artists and presented and discussed their work. Next, Jordahl's students created a trial in which Boy Willie and Berniece, the two principal characters in *The Piano Lesson*, sued one another for the right to decide the future of the piano. Students played the parts of attorney, witnesses, jury, Willie, and Berniece. Judge Jordahl presided. A relatively common activity, classroom trials can often prove perfunctory and superficial. In this case, however, the trial gave students a chance to speak out with energy and commitment in favor of their convictions. Discussions took place throughout the semester, both informally and by using discussion protocols such as the Final Word, the Socratic Seminar, and Interpretation Circles (see "For the Classroom"), and gave them ways to connect the world of the text to their own lives, interests, and concerns.

Much of what students did adhered to the school's standard ninth grade curriculum, modified to focus on the Essential Question and to incorporate a wide range of activities. In Anthony Jacobs's class, for example, students practiced for the state writing exam by responding to several prompts that drew on Inheritance Project themes. One writing prompt read:

A high school student who wants to buy a car suddenly inherited a valuable family heirloom from a grandparent. The student can either sell the heirloom and buy a car or keep the family heirloom to, one day, pass on to their children. What advice would you give this student on what to do with the inheritance and why?[23]

Students' responses to the prompt provided a rich reservoir of material for an ongoing consideration of the semester's essential question. They used repeated reading, improvisation, and discussion to create performances that showed what they knew and were able to do.

For English language learners, the payoff may be especially positive. Making ideas visible through a range of symbol systems and art forms provides a way of rendering those ideas clear, memorable, and explicit. Performance work serves as a bridge to focus stamina and growth of student literacy skills. English language learners and others unfamiliar with the language in books have an opportunity to hear it, see it, and practice it in ways they find interesting and meaningful. They learn to *code switch*—to speak in book language as well as home language. Students see reasons to read. Their contributions become essential to others in the class who are counting on them to understand and contribute. Expectations are explicit. Skills that may otherwise be invisible become visible. The text comes to life.

Comprehension: "Make It Your Own"

If they find the process of taking and using the information, concepts, themes, and examples meaningful, students and class members are likely to want to make something new, turning comprehension into a two-way street. With the support and help of teachers and artists, they learn to create a personal response, practice their work, present it to an audience, receive feedback, reflect on what they've learned, and set goals for the future.

Between early February, when they were introduced to *The Piano Lesson*, and late May, when school ended, students' responses to the question, "What will I do with the inheritance I received?" ranged from the most literal and concrete to the individual and deeply personal. Some students created and performed a "living family tree" of the characters in *The Piano Lesson*. Others followed one character throughout the play in order to understand and explain to others what that character wanted and, in the end, achieved. Many read sections of the play and rehearsed and presented those sections in pantomime. Still others interviewed peers on a variety of topics related to inheritance and made PowerPoint presentations and videos. Yet others composed and presented songs.

As the final assignment of the year, students in several classes wrote personal research papers in a format known as an I-Search paper that addressed the question, "What have I inherited?"[24] Teacher Clara Hutchinson phrased the assignment this way: "Think about Doaker and how much he knew about his family inheritance. Can you tell the story of your family inheritance the way Doaker did?" Offering a personal example,

Hutchinson described how little she knew about her family's tradition of taking a weekly sauna. On the assignment sheet, Hutchinson asked students to interview family or community members, research in books and online, and then "write a research paper on something you or your family have inherited and place it in the context of larger historical or cultural events."[25]

Classes brainstormed aspects of their inheritance they wanted to research. Their final papers showed a high level of engagement and effort. Though in many cases, the mechanics and grammatical conventions were nonstandard—that's why many of these students were tracked into this class—Hutchinson pointed out that student response was "unlike any I have ever had before" in the enthusiasm generated and the number of papers completed and turned in. Topics included Native American pow-wows, tall families, gospel music, and reasons Muslim women wear the hijab. Many papers written by Hmong students addressed topics related to their heritage, clothing, and wedding and funeral traditions. Kham Yang, for example, wrote about an essential part of Hmong funerals, the qeej, a bamboo instrument that leads souls to the realm of their ancestors. Other students used the topic to explore the complex relationship between their heritage and their developing identities as adolescents in the United States. Mai Lee Khang, for example, used the assignment to explore the traditions of Hmong shamanism: "I inherited life as being a young Hmong Christian girl. As I grew older I realize that I can be someone other than who I am today. I have so many questions unanswered. Wanting to know about shamanism isn't an easy thing to do but then looking through its backgrounds there so much you can find."[26]

In Matt Shipman's class, as the year drew to a close, students incorporated the topic into their study of poetry. After reading, discussing, and performing poetry, students created books of their own poems, using the assignment and the genre to explore their own inheritance. One student, Firaol Adam, composed a spirited poem about a distinction central to her identity but unfamiliar to most of her peers and teachers.

> *what I represent . . .*
> Even though my country is called
> Ethiopia,
> I still represent Oromia.
> I cover my hair because I'm a true
> Muslim
>
> Who are you to tell me I'm afraid?
> I represent Oromian pride because
> It's on my mind and Oromo blood
> Is my kind.[27]

As Matt Shipman explained, the Oromo, an indigenous African people whose lands lie within the borders of Ethiopia, are engaged in a long-
standing struggle for liberation. Oppressed and exploited by the Ethiopian
government, in the past twenty years the Oromians have suffered greatly
and migrated in large numbers to Minnesota, where they constitute the
largest Oromian community in the world outside of their home country.

Student responses to Inheritance Project assignments, while not gram-
matically perfect, were substantial and sincere. Students in ninth grade
classes, confident in all that they had learned, were able to *use* the assignments in ways that genuinely mattered. Beginning with their study and
performances of *The Piano Lesson* and other texts and continuing through
the exploration of their own inheritance, students read and wrote to comprehend in the fullest sense of the word. They reached out to grasp information and ideas and took them in hand. They pondered questions
about inheritance, engaged with the themes in the text, and were inspired
to create responses that they shared publicly with their peers, family, and
community. What they learned in these classes became their inheritance,
which they accepted, used, and prepared to pass on.

In summary, these teachers and students, along with visiting artists and
older peers, made great strides in redefining what it means to comprehend.
Together, they moved beyond approaching comprehension as a matter of

recalling characters, retelling plots, understanding vocabulary, or mastering conventions. While these important skills are not in themselves trivial, they do not represent the heart of comprehension, the reason people read, write, speak, and listen. As a community of learners, this remarkable group of educators and students began to shift the focus from the superficial to a deeper, interactive, more personal means of comprehending texts. They gave serious attention to the texts produced by others and recognized that they too could create texts that were both meaningful and significant to themselves and to their communities.

FOR THE CLASSROOM

COMPREHENDING TEXT

Extensive and Intensive Reading

As with any other skill, learners become proficient readers through ongoing practice. Students show a huge variety in the amount and types of reading they do. For most students, reading they do by choice and for pleasure is vastly different from reading assigned by teachers for academic classes. While students are always likely to view these two types of reading differently, teachers can do a great deal to make academic reading interesting and manageable.

- Think carefully about the different types of reading proficient readers do and what it means to be proficient reader of all texts, including print.
- Learn as much as they can about their students' reading interests, habits, and skills.
- Design instruction that incorporates what we know about how best to help students become more proficient readers.
- Establish expectations and a set of guidelines for reading to share with students.
- Encourage students to read both in and out of school and find ways to cross boundaries between in-school and out-of-school reading.

To be proficient, readers need to engage in both wide, or extensive, reading and close, or intensive, reading. From the perspective of an individual student, therefore, we think about reading in terms of *place* (in and out of school) and *type* (extensive or intensive).

By considering reading practices from the perspective of an individual reader in each of these four categories, teachers can make their expectations and their instruction clear and explicit for both their students and themselves. While outlining detailed and specific instructional practices in each of the four categories above is beyond the scope of this book, we offer an overview of possibilities in each of the four categories (see figure 4.1).

- *Intensive reading in school.* Establish *reasons to read* by creating final performances that include portions of a challenging text. Give students a chance to hear the text read aloud by a skilled reader, to practice reading with a partner or small group, to learn the meaning of key vocabulary words, to act out their text using activities such as tableaus or improvisations like Boal's Forum Theatre mentioned in chapter 2, and to engage in discussions like Final Word (described below).
- *Extensive reading in school.* Find out how much time students are spending in uninterrupted reading throughout the school day. (Research suggests surprisingly little.) If your school sets aside time for silent reading, find out how effectively your students are making use of that time and how they are being assisted in learning to use it well. Create classroom libraries and systems for borrowing books. Design systems and times for students to recommend books to one another. Give students time, reasons, and instructions to browse and gather data on a specific topic related to an assignment or planned performance. Invite older students or volunteers to come into your class to discuss texts. Use discussion structures such as Socratic Seminars, Interpretation Circles, or Harkness Discussions (see below).
- *Intensive reading outside of school.* Learn as much as possible about how your students accomplish out-of-school reading assignments and what

FIGURE 4.1
Types of reading

Intensive reading in school	Intensive reading outside of school
Extensive reading in school	Extensive reading outside of school

they can tell you about their successes and challenges. Begin with short, interesting, and relatively easy assignments. Preteach challenging vocabulary. Be sure they are accountable for completing assignments, if possible in ways that help the classroom community create and give performances. Ask them for information on how they manage the time and place for completing the assignment. Establish connections with parents and keep them informed.

- *Extensive reading outside of school.* Learn as much as possible about what and how much students read outside of school. Establish some expectations and accountability for reading that is consistent with giving them as much choice as possible. Ask students what they can tell you about their successes and challenges in selecting and reading books and other material. Establish connections with parents and keep them informed.

Final Word

Final Word provides a structure for students to choose portions of a text they find interesting, meaningful, or significant and have discussions with others about their selected text. Its purpose is to help students make personal connections and explore the theme(s) of the text. Working in small groups of four to seven students, each person chooses and marks a short selection of a text that he finds meaningful or significant and that he would like to hear the group discuss. One person begins the discussion by reading aloud his own selection without commenting on it. One by one, moving around the circle, everyone else comments on the selection. In the end, the person who read the selection has the final word, explaining the significance of this selection and commenting on it. Repeat the process beginning with the next person's selection, everyone commenting on it, and the reader having the final word.

Socratic Seminar

The Socratic Seminar is another text-based and student-centered discussion structure or protocol named after Socrates's belief that by engaging thoughtfully in discussing a topic, individuals will find their way to increased understanding. Therefore, the seminar is designed to foster thoughtful whole-class discussions. While you may create the structure and guidelines, in the discussion you are mainly a listener. The discussion focuses on a text the group has read and begins with a question proposed by you or a member of the group. Though many variations are possible, in the most common design, the class divides in half. Members of the inner circle conduct the discussion, responding to the initial question and supporting their opinions with evidence from the text. Members of the outer circle observe, take notes, and offer feedback on the content and progress of the discussion itself. Often outer circle members have specific tasks to complete as they watch the discussion. One, for example, might be asked to summarize four or five of the points that the student considers most important; another might be asked to count the number of times each inner circle member participates in the conversation. After the outer circle reports their findings, those in the circles change places, take up their assigned roles, and continue the conversation. In addition to providing a structure for full participation for everyone in the class, this protocol gives students an opportunity to reflect on both the content and questions being discussed and the process of taking part in a productive discussion.

Harkness Discussions

The Harkness Discussion, developed at Phillips Exeter Academy, is a method of conducting and evaluating a group discussion led mainly by students as a team effort based on criteria agreed on in advance. The purpose is for students to prepare thoroughly, to think carefully about the topic, and to share their thinking effectively in conversation with others. Responding to questions agreed on in advance, students work together to carry out a discussion in which everyone contributes to illuminate many aspects of a topic; to summarize, restate, and clarify key points; to interpret, analyze, and make connections across texts. The teacher's role is to listen carefully and to track the discussion, to contribute occasionally, and, finally, to evaluate the discussion, giving the entire group one grade for the quality, range, and depth of the discussion.

Many variations are possible. By filming and watching the discussion, for example, students can observe their own contribution as well as the contributions of others and reflect on how future conversations can be improved.

Interpretation Circles

As mentioned in the introduction, Brazilian educator Paulo Freire pioneered the idea of literacy circles as a way of raising the literacy level of poorer communities in Brazil. He opposed the idea of college-educated "experts" traveling to low-income areas to teach others how to read. Rather, he encouraged the development of teachers within communities to form literacy groups using the full range of resources in the community.

Inspired by Freire's literacy circles, Kurt developed this structure for reaching a deep understanding of text by calling on the ideas of the students rather than on the expertise of the teacher. The structure itself necessarily takes the teacher out of the equation and encourages what we refer to as a *density of discourse*. When we talk, we simultaneously are processing and crystallizing our ideas. Therefore, it makes sense to encourage students to engage in as much purposeful talk in the classroom as we can. During interpretation circles, half of the class talks while the other half listens.

1. Interpretation Circles can be used with any texts, fiction or nonfiction. Ask the students to reread a section of the text and instruct them to choose *one* sentence or phrase from the text that they think is most critical for understanding the text You might increase the focus of the activity by asking them to address one of the following questions: What segment do they think is most important? What segment do they personally connect to? What sentence or phrase confuses them? Where do they need the most help? Where do they see images from the text in their heads?
2. Students gather in an open space to stand in a large circle.
3. Everyone counts off by twos around the circle.
4. The 2s form an inner circle facing the outer circle. Each person is now looking at a partner. (If an odd number, form one group of three.)

5. At your direction, each person shares his line or phrase with his partner, and the pair has a conversation about that phrase. If they are focusing on areas of confusion, the pair helps each other figure out what the text might mean. At your signal, the pair takes up the other person's phrase and continues the conversation.

6. In pairs, they now exchange lines with their partner.

7. The outer circle moves one to the right.

8. The process continues with each person now building on the previous conversation and discussing the phrases selected by the previous partner. This allows each person to discuss a range of phrases throughout the process.

9. When everyone returns to their seats, facilitate a discussion about what the students learned from each other. At this point, the air should be thick with ideas.

10. After the conversation you might ask the students to select a key line or phrase and write about their understanding of it in relation to the larger text.

Students can carry out this activity seated in the classroom by switching seats for each conversation. When Interpretation Circles work well, the classroom hums with conversations, and the teacher stands on the side, listening and learning.

Choral Readings

Students work in small groups to prepare and read a small section of assigned text chorally. This activity can be used at any point in the comprehension process to give students a chance to practice reading and rereading a text. This type of close reading and repeated practice promotes fluency (the ability to read automatically, accurately, and expressively). It is especially useful when students are likely to find the text dense and complex. Its purpose is for students to work on fluency, using the rhythms, structures, and conventions of the text so that these become automatic and students can concentrate on constructing meaning.

To begin, each student should have a copy of the text she is to prepare and read, either directly from a book or as an excerpted, enlarged photocopy.

Divide students into groups of four to six and give all performers in each group copies of a selection of text and a set of directions. The directions are a way of inspiring different ways of reading the text.

For your performance include

- A portion of the text read chorally (in unison) by all members of the group
- A portion read by individual members of the group
- One or more portions that you choose to repeat either with individual voices or chorally. The repeats can be a single word, phrase, or sentence.

Consider pacing, speed, and emphasis. Also consider how and where group members want to position themselves during the reading for best effect. Students decide on how to present their selections and rehearse until they are able to give a clear, vivid presentation.

5

Creating Text

Original Energy

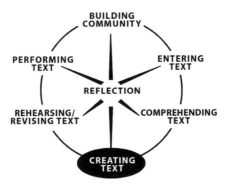

The correct analogy for the mind is not a vessel that needs filling, but wood that needs igniting.

—PLUTARCH

AS THE CLASS BEGAN, a group of five students entered the room and slumped into their chairs. "Anthony's not here. We can't do anything with our poem today."

The class was part of Brown Summer High School, a month-long, low-cost summer enrichment program for Providence-area high school students. Brown Summer High School served as the ArtsLiteracy Project's lab school, a venue where literacy teachers and artists gathered to develop and share ways to develop curriculum based on the Performance Cycle.

This summer, teacher-artist partnerships in eight classrooms worked with Walt Whitman's poem "Song of Myself" as the core text. Teaching partners Kurt Wootton and Brazilian educator Daniel Soares organized their class into small groups, each group rotating through *studios* using different media to address the question, "How do artists represent themselves through their art?"

On this day, from the moment Kurt and Daniel's group entered the classroom, the lethargy was obvious. Nicole announced that she was "anti-Whitman." Kurt asked individual students to read aloud but no one volunteered. Noting how hesitant everyone was, Daniel suggested reading as a group with different people jumping in. "We can't read that way. You need to assign the lines." "Let's just try it and see what happens," Daniel responded. Tentatively, the reading began.

> Afoot and light-hearted, I take to the open road
> Healthy, free, the world before me
> The long brown path before me, leading wherever I choose.[1]

Sometimes individually, sometimes as a chorus, they read. All the students participated except Nicole. As students heard the words read aloud, they picked up their pace. The enthusiasm increased. The result was surprisingly beautiful. One by one, students inquired about the meaning of words like *afoot, allons,* and *camerado,* then mulled over the meaning of the poem itself.

"Let's read the poem again, and this time I'll record it," Kurt offered. The students, at this point, knew the vocabulary and had offered some interesting interpretations. Kurt wanted them to move from *taking* the text to *using* it to create their own work.

They read the poem for a second time. Kurt played it back on the big speakers in the room and everyone listened carefully.

"Let's try it again," someone said. "We can make it better. I messed up."

"Let's plan out who will talk when," Rebecca suggested.

With pens in hand, they marked up the text and assigned lines. This time everyone volunteered to read, even Nicole.

Again, they recorded and listened to their reading. No one was sure what to do next until Josh suggested adding beats to it.

"Great. Bring them in!" Kurt encouraged.

With the recorder in front of him, Josh put his hand up to his mouth to begin, then laughed and turned away from the group. After several tries, he produced a brief series of beats. Everyone clapped and Kurt played back the twelve-second segment of Josh beatboxing.

"I can take the recordings home and edit them using Garage Band," Ricky volunteered.

"Great. Josh, can we get more from you, so Ricky has something to work with?" Kurt asked.

After a few laughing starts, Josh launched into a beat that lasted about four minutes. Exhausted, he then collapsed on the floor. "My mouth is dry. I'm getting some water."

When he returned to the classroom, his beats were playing on the sound system, and the students added the choral reading on top of it.

Josh suggested, "Let's present this to the rest of the class when they come in."

When the whole class gathered, Josh described how they created the piece, then played the digital audio performance. Several students expressed interest in taking the recording home to edit on their computers. One student said, "We want to do that with *our* poems. Can we?"

ESTABLISHING A CREATIVE ENVIRONMENT

When students ask to create new work in response to the topic under discussion, we teachers know we are on the right track. A request of this sort demonstrates the engagement of receptive minds, as well as students' desire to build on their learning by creating something new. As Daniel Pink argues, we are moving from an *information age* to a *conceptual age*. Beyond logical, sequential thinking, new skill sets will require "artistry, empathy, taking the long view, pursuing the transcendent."[2] Similarly, Richard Florida calls today's economy "fundamentally a Creative Economy," pointing to the job growth of the creative workforce and the increase of corporate spending on research and development as strong evidence for his claim.[3] In order to help students prepare for this new world, educators need to emphasize creativity and link it directly to the development of multiliteracies.

Yet, over the last few decades our public schools have steadily moved away from supporting creativity in teaching and learning. The emphasis on assessing student achievement strictly in terms of the narrow measures contained in standardized tests of basic skills creates a press toward a classroom environment that, ironically enough, may reduce rather than foster motivation, one in which *literacy* and *numeracy* are defined as the ability to get the right answer on the test.

Cathy Davidson points out that as a society we are suffering from "attention blindness" by assessing our students in such a narrow way. She describes a mismatch between our education policies and the wide range of abilities students bring into the classrooms. Using the language of the digital age she explains,

> It's as if we're still turning out assembly-line kids on an assembly-line model in an infinitely more varied and variable customizing, remixed, mashable, user-generated, crowdsourced world. As long as we define [student] success by a unified set of standards, we will continue to miss their gifts, we will not challenge their skills, and, in the end, we will lose them from our schools.[4]

Paulo Freire similarly warns against an emphasis on standardization as a "bureaucratizing of the mind" and argues that such an approach asphyxiates "freedom itself and, by extension, creativity and a taste for the adventure of spirit."[5]

In recent years, both time and budgets for school arts programs have been subject to drastic cuts. While the No Child Left Behind legislation of 2001 identifies the arts as one of the ten core academic subjects, the combination of budget cuts and increased emphasis on standardized tests in multiple-choice formats has decimated arts programs, especially in secondary schools. Such testing fails to acknowledge the importance of the range of literacies necessary in the world beyond the schoolroom walls. The ability to observe closely and document carefully, analyze designs and processes, create original and innovative work using a range of symbol systems, make informed judgments about one's work and the work of others, collaborate with peers in designing, creating, and assessing projects— these attributes, omitted from national tests, represent critical skills for success in today's world.

It is possible to achieve a balance between establishing a foundation of content knowledge and skills measurable by standardized tests and providing an environment for innovation and creativity supported by the initiative and originality of both teachers and students. Both kinds of school experiences are essential if we are all to expand our capacities to think broadly about this complex, changing world.

The Brown Summer High School is an environment designed to encourage teachers to explore varied approaches to supporting student literacy development. One summer, in all eight ArtsLiteracy classrooms, teacher-artist partners taught Walt Whitman as the core text and brought other texts to the classroom to share, encouraging students to do the same. All teaching teams adopted several other elements in common. They used the Performance Cycle as an organizing structure for developing an original curriculum. They designed their work around the Essential Question— How do artists represent themselves through their art?—and they agreed that at the culmination of the program, each class would present a public performance to demonstrate what they had learned. They also scheduled afternoon professional development meetings in which teacher-artist teams shared their curricula with one another.

When students read Whitman, they studied the Preface to *Leaves of Grass,* where, 150 years ago, he called for a new poetry to represent the people of the United States: "Of all nations the United States with veins full of poetical stuff most needs poets and will doubtless have the greatest and use them the greatest . . . [The poet] is the arbiter of the diverse and he is the key. He is the equalizer of his age and land."[6] This period in American literature represented a stark break from European traditions. American vernacular in poetry was embraced and heralded as high art. In an edition of *Leaves of Grass* published near the end of his life, Whitman calls for the next generation of poets, predicting theirs would be "the strongest and sweetest songs yet remain to be sung."[7]

We took Whitman's clarion call for new work seriously and offered it as the rallying cry for both students and teachers. The classrooms weren't restricted only to an exploration of the text. The texts provided inspiration and a jumping-off point for the students to do their own creative work. In classes like Kurt and Daniel's, both teachers and students found their "strongest, sweetest songs" by linking their own texts to *Leaves of Grass* in response to Whitman's call. In their final reflections of the summer, teachers and artists unanimously described the structure and content of the program as offering a model teaching and learning environment.

VIEWING CURRICULUM DEVELOPMENT AS A CREATIVE ACT

When teachers open space in the classroom for creation, they have the potential to become artists along with their students. When they design lesson plans that provide students opportunities to show what they can create as a community, they invite the class to share its various ways of understanding a topic or concept. This paradigm shift is liberating and generative for teachers and students alike. Indeed, when veteran teacher Len Newman began to collaborate with artists and to design a curriculum using multiliteracies that included a wide range of art forms, he said, "My repertoire expanded. I began to see my work as more connected to creating. There have been times when I have felt as if I were painting."

In ArtsLiteracy classrooms at Brown Summer High School, teachers were alert to the funds of knowledge and potential contributions of the classroom community. Kurt and Daniel approached their students intent on learning what they had to contribute. Recognizing that their students came from a different generation and from diverse cultural backgrounds, they knew that students were likely to have interesting and unique insights into Whitman's poetry. Although they started with a general structure for the class—students would read, discuss, and respond to the poem by Whitman and develop a shared reading in the form of a performance—they expected to draw on student knowledge, skills, and interests as the work progressed.

Fostering a creative environment means laying a basic foundation in the classroom that encourages students to seek alternative, even unexpected, solutions. We built that environment on five core principles that truly prepare students for life in a diverse and changing world.

Draw on Students' Experiences and Rich Cultural, Intellectual, and Artistic Resources

Students come from a wide range of intellectual and cultural traditions. They bring to the classroom distinctive ways of thinking and communicating. Often, teachers fail to take into account students' backgrounds, experiences, and worldviews. Argentinean educator Emilia Ferreiro describes education that fails to honor students' heritage, experience, and interests as a way of "homogenizing children, despite their original differences" in order to build, "a single people, a single nation."[8] In the United States, this impulse is behind the state and local referenda that call for monolingual cities or the elimination of bilingual schools and programs. Recently, the U.S. National Anthem was translated, sung in Spanish, and widely disseminated on the Internet. The result was a vigorous debate: Should legislation mandate that the National Anthem be restricted to English?

American classrooms include a growing percentage of students from around the world. The recent census points to sharp demographic shifts in the population of both rural and urban areas. The Pew Hispanic Center reports:

The 2000 [United States] census marked the Hispanic population at 35.3 million people, an increase of 58% over 1990. Since then, growth has continued at a brisk pace. The total Hispanic population in 2004 was 40.4 million. That is a jump of more than 14% in just four years; meanwhile the non-Hispanic population was up by barely 2%.[9]

Honoring diversity in the classroom and attending to students' rich funds of knowledge, teachers can build stronger classroom communities by fostering creativity. In addition to the knowledge resulting from cultural diversity, many students possess technological knowledge that surpasses that of their teachers.

Students enter classrooms with multiliteracies that combine media, technologies, and cultures. At home they often create highly sophisticated content that crosses national, economic, and linguistic boundaries in dramatic, often ingenious ways. Yet sadly, as Sonia Nieto notes, "there seems to be a curious refusal on the part of many educators to accept as valid the kinds of knowledge and experiences with which some students come to school, and this is particularly the case with students from low-income and bicultural backgrounds."[10]

When we establish classrooms as spaces for creation and communication, we open possibilities that embrace different ways of seeing the world and communicating meaning. By harnessing the creative energy of students who are talented writers and actors, for example, we create bridges between the resources they bring to classrooms and discipline-based knowledge. In Brown Summer High School, we might have stated as our goal: "Students will read, discuss, and understand the language and ideas in Whitman's 'Song of Myself.'" However, these adult-generated goals rarely acknowledge the backgrounds, skills, interests, and perspectives on learning students possess. Josh decided to put a beat behind Whitman, and suddenly the text leapt off the page. The poem gained an aural and physical texture that gave it freshness and vitality.

Josh's ability to beatbox, Ricky's passion for "all things Mac," and Rebecca's leadership in the choral reading determined how the class approached and interpreted Whitman. Kurt and Daniel consistently provided space for their students to bring their interests to the task at hand. For instance, they introduced a daily opening routine, Call and Response (see "For the Classroom"). Initially, the teachers came to class with a list of key words and phrases from the text. The students gathered in a circle, the teacher called out a phrase, and everyone repeated it with the same level of energy. So, for example, Daniel stepped into the circle and whispered, "Stop this day and night with me" and the students responded quietly. He whispered again, "You shall listen to all sides" and the students repeated it. Then he filled the room with his voice: "I celebrate myself." The room then reverberated with the students' voices.

After a time, Daniel and Kurt asked, "Who would like to lead Call and Response tomorrow?" Students volunteered to study the text and plan their own call and response, adding their own style to the activity. Many students had an interest in hip-hop. On the days that they led, the classroom turned into a concert of Whitman's poetry, with phrases moving back and forth between the MC and the audience. Eventually, a group of students prepared a Call and Response that became the opening for the final performance. On the stage of the Brown University auditorium, three students called out Whitman's lines, and the entire audience of three hundred high school students responded, some even standing and waving their fists in the air as they called out the words, "I sound my barbaric yawp."[11]

Be Alert to the Unexpected

For the past decade, Chicago Arts Partnerships in Education (CAPE) has been creating large-scale, long-term partnerships among Chicago schools, arts organizations, teachers, and artists. In a recent seminar for teachers, Arnold Aprill, CAPE's founding director, showed a slide of a row of student-drawn hand turkeys that appear every November in the halls of elementary schools across America. To create these hand turkeys, students trace their hands on a piece of paper and add turkey qualities: a thumb becomes a head and the fingers the feathers. Students cut out their hand turkeys, and the teacher arranges them in neat rows on the hallway's bulletin board. Commenting on the slide, Aprill said, "This is not the kind of art-making we want to see in our schools. The results are boring and completely predictable."

Our schools suffer from the hand turkey syndrome. By placing too great an emphasis on standardized tests, we teach students to guess what the test maker or teacher is thinking. We close the classrooms to the new and original. In art making and in literacy experiences, we need to facilitate classrooms that provide space for the unexpected. Teaching to the unexpected means that when we, as teachers, introduce a project, paper, or assignment, we don't know what the final product will look like. Teachers succeed when each work reflects individuality. We fail when they all read or look exactly the same.

At the high school level, the emphasis on the five-paragraph essay stands as one of the clearest examples of this failure. Students learn that a well-structured paper consists of an introduction, ending in a single-sentence thesis statement; three body paragraphs, each incorporating a specific idea related to the thesis; and a conclusion that summarizes everything that preceded "in a new way." This format results in a stack of papers often painful to read. More often than not they are plodding, banal, and empty of significant content, valuing form over substance. Who in the real world writes like this? (Note, for example, how many one-sentence thesis statements lead off articles in *The New Yorker*!) A well-written essay contains the number of paragraphs needed to tell the story or express the intended ideas. When we introduce students to a range of authors and examine differences in approaches and styles, we nurture a rich environment for expression and help them gain writing skills in which form follows content, and they focus on what they wish to communicate.

When Kurt and Daniel asked students to write their own *Song of Myself*, they began by helping students generate ideas for their poems. One day they asked, "What is something you are really good at?" Students walked around the space in the configuration of the Human Atom, found a partner, and talked to one another (see chaper 2's "For the Classroom"). The teachers then asked, "What's the story behind what you're good at? How did it happen?" Again, the students walked around the room, found another partner, and shared their answers. "Did someone help you? How did you first get involved in it?" The students continued to change partners and talk about that aspect of themselves. Then they sat down and wrote, incorporating pieces of the story they'd been telling. Eventually, they had several pages of rough notes to work from. Kurt demonstrated how they might use selections from their notes to generate a poem. When students asked, "How long does it have to be?" Kurt answered, "It's your poem. It's a poem about you. Whitman needed to write a poem about himself, and he worked on it over many decades. So take the time you need, and make it as long as you think it should be." Each student produced a unique poem, ranging from one page to more than twenty, but each engaged the reader because the poem genuinely expressed the student's interests, passions, and world outside the classroom.

Teaching to the unexpected produces difficulties. When the products are not uniform, teachers may struggle with assessment. We must have genuine conversations with one another and with students about what constitutes high-quality work. We must be much more creative in our teaching, because for students to create interesting work, they must be inspired. It is our job to light that initial spark by creating *thick air* through the range of materials, texts, and ideas we bring to the classroom environment.

Inspire: Create Thick Air

In the Performance Cycle, we place Creating Text after Building Community, Entering Text, and Comprehending Text. In order for students to create, the classroom must offer safety and support. The students need to be willing to collaborate and to view their peers as colleagues. When students create collaboratively, ideas flow among them and the students gain inspiration from each other's work. In addition, students must be inspired. Entering Text activities engage and spark student interest. Further, they need material to work from. As they interact with texts, they learn about the world beyond their lives, from other times, places, and cultures. Students learn how writers address questions, craft texts, develop themes, and address audiences. Finally, with a classroom full of models and ideas, the creative work can fully begin.

In the Brown Summer High School classroom, the class read much of Whitman's work. After the class discussed a poem, the teachers did what we call *turning a line* back to the students. For example, the teachers took an essential line of a Whitman poem, "I celebrate myself," and asked the students to write beginning with that line. The line turns from Whitman's world to the world of the students. Daniel built an entire language course in Brazil on this simple idea of turning a line and brought this same approach to his classrooms at Brown Summer High School.

Kenneth Koch used a similar technique in which he introduced poems to students and asked them to write their own based on a given poem's structure or concept. He did this, he explained, to "give them experiences which would teach them something new and indicate new possibilities for their writing."[12] To inspire students to think deeply about their lives, they must first develop a perspective that allows them to think through the eyes of another person. They need to be inspired, in Koch's words, to "imagine new possibilities."

Although students start at the same point—with a line, concept, or structure—they produce unique projects in part because the teacher has created thick air. Daniel does not start class by asking his students to take out a pencil and write a poem. He first begins by orchestrating discussions based on prompts he has devised. In one class, students received slips of paper that included one of the following prompts:

- Is there a time when you wanted to explore something—an idea, a hobby, a place?
- When did you feel as though you were trapped?
- When did you feel a need to escape a particular situation or place?
- Was there a time when you had an adventure with a friend, perhaps when you were a child, maybe during summer vacation, maybe in your own house?

With a question in hand, each person found a partner, shared and responded to his prompt, then listened to his partner's prompt and response. Next, partners traded prompts and continued the process with another partner. Daniel asked students to change partners often and to address different questions. By interacting with other students and listening to their responses, the students thought of new possibilities for their own stories.

The class then read Whitman's "Song of the Open Road." The students discussed the ideas in the poem and participated in a freewriting activity. About an hour into the ninety-minute class, with the room filled with words, images, ideas, and stories, Daniel asked the students to begin to write.

Create Clear Organizing Structures

Teaching to the unexpected does not mean that teachers enter the classroom without a structure. Quite the opposite. Structures provide opportunities for students to create original work. Organization involves attention to both time and space in the classroom. Nancie Atwell's writing workshop, described in several of her books, including her best-known *In the Middle*, provides a helpful model of a classroom community structured for creating.[13] She begins the class with a mini-lesson to inspire students and to offer concrete tools for writing. She may read a poem from a student or a published author, give a lesson on first lines, or suggest ideas for revising work. Students then have time to write stories, poems, or essays. At the end of class they share their work without judgment. By sharing original work, students informally publish their writing, and other writers in the class encounter texts that may inspire future work. By sharing authentic work, every class ends with a sense of surprise.[14]

At Brown Summer High School, Kurt and Daniel arranged the physical structure of the classroom into arts studios. They set up spaces in the classroom for students to interpret Whitman's text through different artistic mediums: sound, photography, film, and performance. The students cycled through different studios, working in each medium to develop their own unique products demonstrating their understanding of Whitman's text. Kurt and Daniel appointed student leaders for each studio to give the teachers more freedom to move from group to group to coach when needed.

In each studio, they used Atwell's structure as a general guide. In the photography studio, the students began with a ten-minute mini-lesson on the digital camera. Then, Jessica Delforge, a Brown student assistant, showed images of a project from photographer Wendy Ewald's book *Secret Games*.[15] Ewald, an award-winning teaching artist, works with different populations in various parts of the world. Her students' compelling photographs have been published in books and exhibited in museums. The group looked at the self-portraits of students in *Secret Games* and then discussed how they wanted to frame their own portraits. Jessica explained to the students, "In the other classrooms you are making a 'Song of Myself' using writing, just like Whitman. Here you don't have words, only images. How will you convey who you are in just three images?"

In small groups, students left the building to explore different spaces they might choose as the setting for their photographs. When they returned twenty minutes later, Jessica passed out notecards. "Now instead of moving immediately to taking photographs, I'd like you to think about what you are trying to convey about yourself in the photograph." In all of these activities, Jessica wanted students to: (1) learn some tools of the trade by examining others' photography; (2) examine and discuss the environment they would choose to photograph; and (3) consider what they wanted to communicate in their photographs. Finally, at the end of the class, students read their notecards to each other, sharing their ideas.

The next day in class Jessica repeated the structure. She began with a ten-minute mini-lesson, a quick demonstration of how to use the camera to focus on a subject and control the light, then handed a camera to each group. Students went to the sites they had preselected and took three self-portraits. When they returned to the classroom twenty minutes later, they shared their photographs across groups.

The daily lesson design consisted of three repeated components:

1. *The mini-lesson.* The teacher selects specific published photographs to illustrate a particular point, or she introduces "tools of the trade," teaching students how to use a camera.

2. *Studio time.* The students work independently or in groups on their own ongoing processes. The teacher circulates and coaches.
3. *Sharing or performing.* Students share their work with one another. Often the work will be in-process, and group members will describe their own processes and offer possibilities for moving forward.

Encourage the Use of Multiple Mediums

When students create text, they rewrite, recreate, remix, and recycle their work. As cultural critic Edward Said writes,

> Yes, we need to keep coming back to the words and structures in books we read, but, just as these words were themselves taken by the poet from the world and evoked from out of silence in the forceful ways without which no creation is possible, readers must also extend their readings out into the various worlds each one of us resides in.[16]

Creating through various art forms extends students' unique readings into the world, so that they actively create rather than passively receive.

In Kurt and Daniel's class, Whitman's text was—to use the digital term—remixed, or, in Freire's words, re-created several times through different mediums of art making.[17] The first remixing occurred when students read the text for the first time. When students read—even when they struggle—words, images, ideas, interpretations enter their minds. This kind of cognitive re-creation occurs every time they reread, as they learn more about a work's context, and as they participate in discussions and hear others' interpretations. To re-create a text, the student and teacher look for possibilities and connections: How do you interpret this line? What might the author have intended? What line do you think is most powerful? Most moving?

The second re-creation occurred when students planned a choral reading. They decided how to turn the text into a soundscape, choosing when a single or many voices would read, when to re-read a line to give it additional emphasis. They determined when a line called for a soft, loud, aggressive, or gentle reading. The third re-creation involved putting a beat behind it. The entire class became an audience as they listened to the taped reading supported by a beatbox rhythm. Finally, Ricky volunteered to take the audio recording home and remix it using the computer program Garage Band. Each remix involved the particular resources of the students who encountered the poem. Eventually this remixed performance became the background for a movement piece in the final performance at the end of the summer, adding yet another layer.

This process of creation and re-creation can occur through any artistic medium. The examples we've mentioned involved writing, photography, visual art, performance, and music. When we reinterpret text through a new medium, we are actively engaging in cognition. We see this process echoed in chemistry. To create a chemical reaction, two reactant substances are combined. The reaction releases energy and yields a new product that often has qualities different from the originals. Similarly, when we integrate text and the arts, we create something new. Students' minds, bodies, and spirits become active as they work to transform the text into a new medium.

This approach differs from the way we traditionally ask students to respond to text in classrooms: by answering comprehension questions, defining unfamiliar vocabulary words, taking quizzes or tests, writing papers, or participating in class discussions. Each of these activities has value, and we are not suggesting teachers avoid them. We are arguing, instead, for a balance to engage students' full capacities and intelligences.

Paulo Freire writes about the transformation of classrooms from authoritarian to dialogic, a process that moves a class from a structure in which teachers dispense information and enforce rules to one in which the students and the teachers explore ideas together and build on one another's words and worlds. In the classrooms we envision, students dialogue not only through words but also through multiple artistic mediums. When the community and the creative process are nurtured—when we create together—we establish a transformational environment that challenges the notions of teacher and student. The students become storytellers, performers, visual artists, dancers, writers, and photographers, and suddenly new capacities and talents emerge.

CELEBRATING ORIGINAL ENERGY

For the final performance of the summer course, Kurt and Daniel slated Josh to begin the presentation by reciting the first lines of "Song of Myself."

During the dress rehearsal, Josh began, "I celebrate myself . . ." He hesitated, looked up at the ceiling and down at the floor. Shaking his head, he walked off stage.

Afterward, Kurt approached him. "Do you want to do this tomorrow? Can you memorize it before tomorrow?"

"Yes. I can do it. I want to do it," Josh replied.

On the day of the performance, Josh stepped out on the stage, alone. No one had seen him successfully perform the opening of Whitman's poem. Parents, brothers and sisters, Brown faculty, graduate students, and high school friends filled Brown's main auditorium in Salomon Hall.

Josh began,

> I celebrate myself, and sing myself,
> And what I assume you shall assume,
> For every atom belonging to me as good belongs to you.

He paused, looked out at the audience with the same worried expression as the day before. He looked over at the side of the stage where Kurt nodded encouragingly. He then launched into the rest of his performance and concluded strongly,

> Creeds and schools in abeyance,
> Retiring back a while sufficed at what they are, but never forgotten,
> I harbor for good or bad, I permit to speak at every hazard,
> Nature without check with original energy.[18]

Josh's performance epitomized what we learned that summer at Brown Summer High School—how to create classrooms vibrant with, in

Whitman's words, an "original energy." As the performance continued, Josh and his classmates presented sections of "Song of Myself" interwoven with their own creative work inspired by Whitman. Photographic self-portraits were projected onto a large screen on stage as students' recorded voices told the stories of their photographs. In small groups and individually, students performed their original poems. Josh and Ricky's remix of Whitman's poem filled the auditorium while a group of students performed a movement piece. The performance stood as an apt metaphor for creating in a community. Conversations between Whitman and the students; conversations among students; conversations between students and the audience—all demonstrated how the past, present, and future blend into an act of creation.

FOR THE CLASSROOM

CREATING TEXT

Center to Edge of Text

A useful construct we've found for moving from comprehending to creating is to consider response and analysis of text as a continuum that moves from the center of the text to the edge of the text.[19] Responses at the center of text are those that directly address interpretations of the text itself. In a language arts classroom they might look like the following questions:

- Why do you think Hamlet doesn't kill his uncle in the middle of the play?
- Why does Kino wait so long to throw away the pearl?

We then move along the continuum to create responses still closely connected to the text, but that involve students' original creative work. These responses involve students adding to or altering the narrative. Students might, for example, imagine what happens after a story ends or insert a "missing" scene. Examples include:

- Write a eulogy for Icarus from the perspective of Daedalus based on Ovid's telling of the story of "Icarus and Daedalus" in *The Metamorphoses*.
- Add dialogue between Esperanza, her sisters, brothers, and her parents as the family prepares to move to the house on Mango Street.

Edge-of-text responses are conceptually tied to the text but extend and expand on the theme, story, or characters, locating it beyond the text and in the wider world. For example:

- In *To Kill a Mockingbird*, students read the section where Scout describes learning to read: "Now that I was compelled to think about it, reading was something that just came to me, as learning to fasten the seat of my union suit without looking around, or achieving two bows from a snarl of shoelaces."[20] Inspired by Scout's account, the teacher asks the students to describe their experiences of learning to read.

- The class reads Ray Bradbury's short story "The Rocket," about a father who dreams of taking his family into space. The students then discuss and write about dreams they have for themselves and for their families.

Turning a Line

Freire emphasizes the importance of the back-and-forth relationship between the word and the world. He emphasizes, "Not a reading of the word alone, nor a reading only of the world, but both together, in dialectical solidarity."[21] We structure our experiences with literature in this way, considering how we might foster a close relationship between the reader and the text. Louise Rosenblatt notes that the text may serve as a mirror with which we might see our own world reflected through the eyes of another: "The reader seeks to participate in another's vision—to reap knowledge of the world, to fathom the resources of the human spirit, to gain insights that will make his own life more comprehensible."[22]

When we are planning to teach a work of literature, one of the techniques we use is turning a line. The previous examples we gave of turning a line were focused on poetry in the classroom—seeing how Whitman's work might help to inspire ideas for writing our own "Song of Myself."

When we selected readings for Brown Summer High School, we read with a pen in hand, marking those sections of the text that might serve as inspiration for students to develop their own work. When Kurt was teaching John Steinbeck's *The Pearl* in Mexico, his class came across the line, "They came to the place where the brush houses stopped and the city of stone and plaster began, the city of harsh outer walls and inner cool gardens where a little water played and the bougainvillea crusted the walls with purple and brick-red and white."[23] This description of a city in Mexico with poor "brush houses" and the wealthier houses with "cool gardens" inspired the students to examine their own city of Merida, to consider the contrasts between various social classes and how those contrasts were revealed in the architecture and physical appearance of neighborhoods. Each student wrote an essay examining contrasts in her own city. They embraced Freire's call to connect the "word to the world" by using the literature to look critically at the social circumstances in their own world.

Call and Response

Developed at Brown Summer High School by Daniel and Kurt, Call and Response models ways to read fluently and with meaning and invites students to participate in an aesthetic reading of a text. For those students who have difficulty with reading, Call and Response provides an opportunity to practice reading a text as a community without being singled out. The activity Call and Response comes out of traditions in the African American church and hip-hop concerts, where vocal participation is encouraged.

Before class, select a list of key phrases or sentences from the designated text. Virtually any lines can work, though the best choices are lines that carry an emotional or aesthetic punch and that are essential to an understanding of the text.

The group gathers in a large circle. Everyone in the room needs to be able to make eye contact with one another. Ask the students to pull their shoulders back, take their hands out of their pockets, and avoid crossing their arms during the vocal warm-up. This will help them to open their voices, to speak with conviction and clarity. Next, walk into the center of the space and call out lines of text. The students repeat the lines back in chorus. Read with emotion, matching the tone of the text and encouraging students to match the energy and quality of the reading.

You might then playfully point to individual students and challenge them to match your level of energy. The warm-up continues with many lines, moving back and forth between you, individual students, and the entire group.

This activity can become a daily ritual in the classroom. As students become comfortable, they can take over the lead, calling out the lines to the rest of the group. It's important for student leaders to review the text carefully beforehand, choosing, marking, and practicing the lines they will lead the class in reading. This makes an excellent and purposeful homework assignment.

In Daniel and Kurt's final performance at Brown Summer High School, the Call and Response became the opening event. An entire class stood on the stage in a U formation. Standing in the center, three student leaders called out lines from Whitman. The class, and eventually the entire auditorium, repeated the lines in response. The class then added a Brazilian choral melody, accompanied by a guitar, between the calls and responses: "I celebrate myself . . . and sing myself."

Rapid Brainstorming

Rapid Brainstorming is a process developed by Jan Mandell for helping students find ideas for writing. When Jan taught at Brown Summer High School, we documented how she led this process in the classroom.

Jan's students each took a piece of paper and pen and sat in a chair or on the floor in a place where they were comfortable. She explained, "There is not a right way or a wrong way to write. This is your life. These are your stories, your words. Write as fast as you can. Don't take your pen off the paper."

Jan then gave students a series of prompts for which they were to write quick lists, allowing a brief time for each topic. The students began writing. After about thirty seconds she instructed, "Stop. Draw a line across your paper. Don't worry if you didn't finish. This is about generating quick ideas. Next topic." She had her students brainstorm in rapid succession the following topics:

- Foods you love to eat
- Images or things in your neighborhood
- Things you did when you were a child, toys you played with, memories, places you went
- Music you like to listen to, music that rocks your mind, settles your soul, music you listen to escape, lyrics from songs that come to you
- Things you love, things you love to do, your grandmother, your best friend, climbing on mountains, taking a vacation, anything that comes to mind

When students finished, Jan explained, "This will be your cheat sheet, the notes you will use. I will give you a poetry prompt. Begin with the words 'I come from.' Use that phrase as often as you like and fill in with words from your lists. Play with it. Add to what you've written. Change it. It just helps to have something to begin with. You have 10 minutes to create a poem."

Students worked silently on their poems using the rough ideas from their rapid brainstorming page. After about ten minutes, Jan instructed the students, "Pick up your paper with the poem on it; get up on your feet; walk around the room; just walk. Now read your poem out loud. Don't worry about anyone around you. Just start reading." Students walked and read their poem aloud.

After a brief time, Jan stopped them and explained, "The next time you walk, I want you to edit the poem down to a size you would be brave enough to share in the room. Choose the parts you want to keep, and those you want to throw out. This is what I call editing on your feet. Take your pen with you. Add something new if you like." Her students walked again, reading their poems and editing as they walked.

Jan instructed, "Find a partner. Introduce yourselves. You're just going to read a little bit of your poem. Choose person A and B. A will read to B. B, please be the most respectful listener on the planet. Make eye contact, I won't let you read for longer than a few seconds. Go." Students read until Jan said, "Switch so that B is reading to A."

Jan then brought the class together in a circle. "First repeat after me 'I' [everyone said 'I' in chorus], 'Come,' [chorus], 'From,' [chorus], 'I Come From,' [chorus]. Now we'll go around the circle and you will share your edited poem with the rest of the class. Read as much of your poem as you are comfortable sharing. For you, maybe that's just one line or one verse, or maybe it's the whole poem. Share any part you want."

That summer in Jan's class, students read the novel *Bless Me, Ultima* by Rudolfo Anaya. After the students read their own poems, and before they began reading the novel, Jan gave an inspiring speech that captured the essence of why we read and why we write:

These are very personal poems. We're doing this as artists, as poets. This is how poets begin writing poems. They begin at the very beginning, by just using basic language, introducing themselves, telling a little bit about their story. And when we get into B*less* M*e*, U*ltima*, you'll hear another person telling a story; and it's a lot more words, and that's the only difference.

Jan's process of rapid brainstorming breaks down inhibitions and encourages innovation. We've used this process in a variety of classrooms when beginning different types of writing from narrative to poetic.

Four-Square Brainstorming

Another process of generating thick air in the classroom was introduced to us by Chicago artist Robert Possehl at the annual Habla Teacher Institute in Merida, Mexico. He presented a complex process for making books as art objects. In order to have some meaningful content to shape the book around, Robert introduced the following activity, Four-Square Brainstorming.

Prior to this exercise, the participants had been exploring the concept of *childhood spaces*. Robert asked them to think of places that were important to them as children. In pairs, they shared their stories. Robert then handed everyone a standard size sheet of paper. He demonstrated, folding the paper in half, then in half again to form four equal parts.

Robert explained, "In the first quadrant write the name of the place from one of the stories you told earlier. When I say *go*, start drawing circles around that word until another word comes to mind. Then quickly write that word and begin drawing circles around the new word until you think of another. Fill the first quadrant up with words and circles. Don't take your pencil off the page. If you can't think of another word, then keep making circles. You have about three minutes. Go!"

In the second quadrant, Robert asked everyone to write an important question someone else might ask about the story, "something that is missing from the story as you previously told it. A very important detail or perhaps some background knowledge that you didn't explain the first time around."

In the third quadrant, Robert asked the participants to focus on the senses. He instructed, "There are five basic senses: seeing, hearing, smelling, tasting, and touching. Write a word for each of those five senses that relates to your story so you will know the story you are telling by just those five words. A sight. A sound. A taste. A texture. A smell."

In the fourth quadrant, he asked everyone to write a headline that captured the essence of the story.

Robert then instructed, "Using all this rough material, take out a fresh sheet of paper and begin to write your story."

Over the years we have added variations to the four quadrants, depending on when and how we have used this tool in the writing process. We have asked students to do the following:

- List the key objects in your story
- Write a mini-dialogue between two characters
- Sketch the setting of your story
- Describe the setting
- Describe one of the major characters in your story
- Describe one of the minor characters in your story
- List the major symbols in your story

6

Rehearsing and Revising

Getting It Right

I believe the work of excellence is transformational. Once a student sees that he or she is capable of excellence, that student is never quite the same. There is a new self-image, a new notion of possibility. There is an appetite for excellence.

—Ron Berger

WHEN EIGHT-YEAR-OLD FLOR first entered the classroom, her teacher, Jessica Robertson, noticed that she purposely avoided other students and sat alone at a table. Jessica's classroom was organized around worktables, each seating about five students. In the first few weeks of class, Jessica tried to help Flor meet other students by putting her in groups or pairs, but to no avail. Each day Flor sat by herself.

Flor's reticence to meet other students reflected her general attitude in the classroom. When asked a question, Flor always responded with a negative comment. When given a writing assignment, Flor quickly wrote one or two words, then put down her pencil. When Jessica tried to coax her to write more, Flor responded, "Acabé" ("I'm done"), in Spanish, her first language.

Jessica knew that Flor's previous teacher, Karla Hernando, had succeeded in winning Flor's participation, so she sent an e-mail seeking advice:

> I'm writing you to ask you about a student I'm worried about. From the time I met her (three weeks ago), Flor has shown absolutely no interest in class. When I ask her questions, she always answers, "I don't know. I don't do anything. I don't like anything. I don't do any activities. I don't have friends. I'm not good at anything." Only negative answers. I try to get her involved. We do drawing, acting—I (and the other students) give her compliments. We tell her she is really good at drawing, that she knows a lot of vocabulary in English; we ask about her opinions, but her answer is always "nothing." So I'm really concerned and I want to find a way to help her get her involved. How was she in your class? Did she express herself in a negative way, or was she different in your class? How did you find a way to get her interested? Even when we paint or draw she says she "doesn't like it" and she sits in silence and stares into space.[1]

Karla and Jessica teach at Habla: The Center for Language and Culture in Merida, Mexico, a school inspired by the ArtsLiteracy Project's work in Brazil and devoted to language learning.[2] Nine years after the founding of ArtsLiteracy in Rhode Island, Kurt Wootton and María del Mar Patrón Vázquez created Habla to further explore ways the arts contribute to literacy and language development. Mexico has a standardized, national curriculum for all its public *and* private schools, none of which offers much room for teaching outside the curriculum. Wootton and Patrón Vázquez opened Habla as an afterschool organization in order to have creative freedom and to pioneer approaches to teaching outside the traditional system. Habla provides arts, language, and literacy classes to students of all ages. (Currently the youngest student at Habla is four years old and the oldest is eighty-six.)

The school employs teaching artists who collaborate with language teachers to integrate the arts into their classrooms. For students of Flor's age, Habla offers year-round English classes and a bilingual summer school modeled on Brown Summer High School. Flor studies English at Habla and participates in both the summer school—where she first met Karla—and in the year-round afterschool language classes, where she works with Jessica as her primary teacher and Karla as a visiting artist.

In the summer program, Flor demonstrated the same reticence to speak and participate that Jessica later described. Karla explained, "Flor was always by herself, always apart from the others. She didn't seem very confident. When she offered ideas in the classroom, they didn't relate to anything anyone else was saying." After the first two classes, she observed Flor in the corner of the classroom drawing. "I walked over to see what she was doing and she was drawing birds. I asked if I could see them. She handed me a notebook. On every page was a beautiful bird. It was incredible." Instead of asking Flor to put her drawings away, Karla praised Flor for her work and her interest. "I wanted to find a way for Flor to bring her birds to the classroom, to make them a part of what we were doing. She felt valued when we took an interest in and praised her birds."

Modeled on the Performance Cycle, each week of Habla's summer program culminates in a performance. The students in Karla's class decided that Flor's birds should be central to the Friday performance. The class was studying the concept of urban spaces and had been discussing the relationship between humans and nature in cities. Karla photocopied each of Flor's birds onto a transparency and, with an overhead projector, projected them onto large sheets of cardboard. Each student chose a bird and traced it onto the cardboard. They then painted the large birds any color they liked, and these became the primary characters in the performance.

Although Flor did become a part of the classroom community in Karla's class, she still rarely spoke in English. With Jessica as her teacher the next semester, Flor returned to familiar patterns. After Jessica sent Karla her e-mail, the two teachers agreed to meet. Together, Karla and Jessica designed a project that lasted the entire semester.

Jessica explained, "At the beginning of the year Flor knew a lot of words in English, but she didn't know how to put them together. This is often the case with many students of this age. They know individual words but aren't able to form sentences or tell a story."[3] Typically, most English classes in Mexican schools are organized around the content of textbooks that require students to memorize vocabulary but rarely challenge them to use the new language to communicate in meaningful ways. The textbooks are filled with games and activities like crossword puzzles, fill-in-the-blank sentences, and picture and word matching exercises; they resemble the coloring books found in the toy section of a supermarket. The students memorize a set of words (numbers, animals, food), play vocabulary games in the classroom, and go home at night to fill out their workbooks. Every few weeks they take a multiple-choice or fill-in-the-blank test on the given vocabulary and are graded on spelling and word meanings. Many students like Flor enter Habla knowing many words, but they lack the skills to put them together into sentences or narratives.

Karla and Jessica knew they needed a different approach in order to reach Flor. Karla explained, "In Flor's other school she said no one paid attention to her. No one cared about what her talents were. When we noticed her birds and made them a big part of the classroom, she felt accepted." Rather than jumping from activity to activity, Jessica and Karla designed an experience that mattered to Flor and the rest of the students, a project that lasted for three months, involved significant revising and rehearsal, and provided space for the students to try things, make mistakes, and work to achieve a substantive result. Rather than receiving a grade for their work, the students presented their final products to their parents and the community at the end of the semester and received written feedback from their teachers.

REHEARSING AND REVISING

In the Performance Cycle, we combine the concepts *rehearsing* and *revising*, terms that have much in common but usually apply to other disciplines.

Rehearsing usually refers to the process of moving toward a performance in theater, dance, or music. It involves repeated practice, experimenting with different approaches, and making changes until a piece is ready to display. *Revising* typically refers to writing. Writers revise—adding, deleting, or reshaping—until satisfied enough to share their work in some form. Both processes have a similar goal: they ask us to commit to working on a particular product over time in order to make improvements. In both writing and performing, these processes can be demanding, often confusing experiments. Professional writers and performers would doubtless agree that success depends on rehearsing and revising. Rarely, if ever, do we get it right on the first try.

We know that our students come to the classroom with unique funds of knowledge and creative capacities, but as Kathleen Cushman's students point out in her book *Fires in the Mind*, students need to engage in *deliberate practice* if they are to move from rough ideas and artistic impulses to high-quality, crafted work.[4] If students present their rough work—the first draft or the monologue read once off the page without commitment—they fail to demonstrate their full capacities. Students need to revise and rehearse in order to develop and show their abundant gifts.

In 2007, the Alliance for Excellent Education conducted a meta-analysis of the teaching techniques considered most effective in helping high school students become better writers. Across all studies, the techniques that had the largest effect on improving student writing were processes related to revision: "Whether generic or highly focused, explicitly teaching adolescents strategies for planning, revising, and/or editing has a strong impact on the quality of their writing."[5] Planning, revising, and editing require time. For students to engage in these processes, they need ample time and encouragement to determine what works and throw away what doesn't. They need to feel that every move they make in their work isn't being graded by their teacher.

Too often, however, students have very little interest in revising or rehearsing. When asked to rehearse for a performance, students might roll their eyes and groan, "Again?" as they take their places on the stage. In writing classrooms, students may dutifully fill out a peer editing work-sheet in a cursory, disinterested way or create a final draft by copying an earlier draft verbatim using neater handwriting. At best, student writers might make a few minor changes before handing in their "completed" work. Our goal as teachers must be to engage students in meaningful work where, as we mention in the comprehension chapter, they have a desire to *make it their own*.

AN ETHIC OF EXCELLENCE

When students own the assignment and care about the quality of their final product, they are much more patient with the process and willing to rehearse and revise to improve their work. Ron Berger, a teacher in rural Massachusetts, works to instill in his students what he calls "an ethic of excellence." In his mind, the "most important assessment that goes on in a school isn't done to students but goes on inside students."[6] In order to motivate students to aim for excellence, Berger shows his class models of exemplary student work from years past, encourages all students to pay attention to and care about one another's work, designs compelling and authentic projects for students to work on in the classroom, and always makes their learning public. As he explains,

> Every final draft my students complete is done for an outside audience.
> It may be for a small audience of kindergarten children or for a national
> audience on educational television. Either way, my role as a teacher is not
> as the sole judge of their work but rather similar to that of a sports coach or
> play director: I am helping them to get their work ready for the public eye.
> There is a reason to do the work well, and it's not just because the teacher
> wants it that way.[7]

Rehearsing and revising instills in students the need to get it right, internalizing a sense of excellence that results in both commitment and stamina.

MATTERING

The more the work matters to the student, the higher the quality of rehearsal and revisions. In their study of exceptional arts programs in ten settings in the United States, Lauren Stevenson and Richard Deasy note the importance of *mattering:*

> "Mattering" was the central concept that teachers, students, and school administrators expressed when they described the impact the arts had on student learning, and why the arts learning experiences engaged students in different and more powerful ways than other school programs. Learning mattered to students, they said, and students felt like they mattered in schools.[8]

For learning to matter, classroom topics and activities must connect to what Maxine Greene refers to as the "lived worlds" of the students—their passions, interests, and experiences.[9] This does not at all mean that teachers should abandon content that students don't find immediately familiar and relevant. Instead, we must create a dynamic interaction between the students' experiences and the discipline being studied. Students need to read outside their immediate worlds; the opportunity to enter other worlds is one of the great virtues of reading. However, such reading will have little meaning and make little impact if students can't bring it to life. Using Jeffrey Wilhelm's felicitous phrase, "You gotta *be* the book."[10] When we help students connect academic content to their worlds, their learning is likely to matter.

When students want to make the work their own, they will engage in a dialogue between their lived worlds and the central text. And when they prepare their completed work to present to others in print or on stage, they will open that dialogue to a conversation with a wider audience. Effective revision/rehearsal does not come from filling out a peer-editing worksheet or measuring work against a rubric that describes an effective performance. Instead, the desire to move their work toward excellence lies at the very core of why we perform and write: to share something of our authentic selves, to be heard and be remembered.

A LAYERED PROCESS

Although Revising/Rehearsing appears in the Performance Cycle immediately before a final performance, the rehearsal and revision process actually begins the first day of class and continues after the cycle ends. After Karla, the teaching artist, received Jessica's e-mail regarding Flor's reticence to participate, Jessica and Karla decided to design a class that encouraged the students to bring their passions to the classroom at the same time they were learning English. Inspired by Dr. Seuss's book *The Lorax*, the teachers designed the class around the concept of *planting seeds*.[11] In *The Lorax*, a character named the Once-ler destroys all the trees in his community in his greed to make more and more money. At the end of the book, the Once-ler has a change of heart and gives a boy—who has been listening to his story of destruction—the last seed for the now-extinct trees and advises,

> It's a Truffula Seed.
> It's the last one of all!
> You're in charge of the last of the Truffula Seeds.
> And Truffula trees are what everyone needs.
> Plant a new Truffula. Treat it with care.
> Give it clean water. And feed it fresh air.[12]

The obvious curriculum might have been shaped around the students planting seeds in the garden, watching them grow, and perhaps journaling about their trees, but Jessica and Karla took a different approach. They discussed with the students what it meant to "grow stories" and "grow the imagination." They also explored with the students how they might "grow language" from the seeds of words. Jessica explained to the class, "Now you know many, many words in English. But it's difficult to find ways to put them together isn't it? We're going to see how we can use the words you have now to make sentences and to tell stories." Jessica explained in an interview, "I wanted them to tell stories that were intricate, using more than just a few words. I knew I needed a stronger structure to guide them through it, so I broke the process down into parts."

She began by reading the students *The Lorax* in English. She encouraged them just to listen to capture the gist of the story. Afterward, she asked if anyone could summarize in Spanish what the story was about. Next, the students drew a timeline across the floor of the classroom and, writing in English, inserted the various events. *The Lorax* begins in the present, jumps back to the past, and then returns to the present. As the students constructed the timeline, they took note of the structure Seuss uses to tell the story.

Jessica then asked, "Stories often have a problem, something that goes wrong, that needs to be resolved. Where do you see the problem in the story?" The students realized that the problem begins in the middle of the timeline, in time past. "Good, the problem is already huge at the beginning, and the story flashes back to the past to show how it began. How do the characters in the story solve the problem?"

Jessica and the students discussed the story's characters. "We talked about how in *The Lorax* there was a good character and a destructive character." She asked the students to think about creating their own stories using the structure of *The Lorax,* starting in the real world, moving to an imaginary world, and ending with a return to the real world.

The students drew pictures of their real and imaginary worlds. Earlier in the semester, they had discussed the idea of *home* and what makes them feel at home. The students used their vision of home as the setting of their real world. Jessica explained, "Flor's home is her room, and the thing that transports her to her imaginary world is being underneath her bed reading *The Field Guide to the Birds of North America.* All of Flor's stories begin and end with birds! Flor includes the things she loves most in her story." Flor was writing something that mattered to her. With Karla's advice, Jessica shaped a project that allowed Flor to build her classroom work around her love of birds.

As she worked on her story, Flor joined the rest of the students in the circle and described the two worlds she had created, the world of her room and her bird world. She was clearly engaged. When Karla visited the classroom, she remarked, "I was amazed to see Flor sharing her ideas in the group. Previously she might listen, but she sat in the circle silent. At the most she would say one or two words. Now she was actually putting entire sentences together."

In the next step in the process, they created two characters. The first—based on the Once-ler—was a destructive character. The second represented the student, similar to the boy who receives the seeds. The students drew sketches of their characters then wrote words describing them. From their words, the class created a word wall that helped everyone find additional words to add to their character descriptions.

Again, students sat in a circle and described their characters. If they saw a relationship or a story emerging between the two characters, they gave a quick summary of their thinking. The students were creating thick air, developing and drawing on ideas and themes that would help them create rich stories. In addition, they were taking the first steps in a process we have come to call *layering*.[13]

A layered experience is one in which the student's work moves across expressive mediums and becomes increasingly complex. They began by drawing pictures of the characters they planned to include in their stories. Next, they chose and wrote down words to describe their images. Then they discussed their images and words in groups, modifying and revising their sketches and descriptions as they continued.

In schools, teachers often teach revision as a corrective process. Students create a draft then "fix" the errors. In contrast, Jessica asked her students to translate their ideas through multiple symbol systems. As students explored different mediums, they built a repertoire of vocabulary, visual images, sounds, and even movement. Revision took place every step of the way.

The students next situated their characters and settings in an actual story. On a large sheet of poster board, each person designed a twelve-part storyboard. Using the structure of *The Lorax*, the students decided that the first two boxes of the storyboard would describe life in the real world. Then, in the next eight boxes the good character, representing the student, would travel to the imaginary world to meet the destructive character and there encounter a problem to solve. Finally, in the last two boxes, the main character would return to the real world.

Rather than using words, the students drew their stories. Jessica explained, "Most of the students first created their real world at the beginning and the real world at the end. They put their problems in the middle and then from there filled in the rest. I went around and coached them. 'What has to happen? Who is this character? What role are you going to have in the story?' Many of the students forgot to put themselves in their story. Flor was not one who forgot. She knew exactly where she was going to be and what role she played."

Jessica then prompted the students to add words to their illustrations. The students wrote key words in each square of their storyboards. They asked for any English words they didn't know.

The class then went outside to participate in an activity called Walking Stories, which allows the author to be his own first reader, to hear a draft of the story spoken out loud. The presence of other writers speaking their stories aloud, and the opportunity to walk as they talk, diminishes the students' self-consciousness and encourages them to create and elaborate as they walk. With storyboards in hand, the students walked across the yard and back telling their stories in English. Jessica urged them to repeat their stories as they crossed the yard, each time telling the stories in a different way. She explained, "The first time I told them just to tell their stories. The second time I told them to tell their stories again and add specific details about the place—what it looked like, the objects they saw and the colors. Then I asked them to think about the characters and the emotions they felt—if they thought the characters were feeling bad, happy, or nervous. Finally, I had them put it all together and tell it one more time."

Each time the students came back from a walk, they asked Jessica for any words they didn't know. For example, when Jessica asked them to think about emotions, one girl asked for the English word for *preocupado* (worried). After walking and telling several versions of their stories, the students returned to the classroom to write.

The first drafts of the stories, rough sketches at best, needed much more development. Jessica explained,

> The next day, to begin the revision process, we thought about sequence words—words to make the story flow better. I had a set of notecards that had all kinds of sequence words on them (*suddenly, later, before, after*, etc.). I introduced them to the group and asked if they could think of any more. As they told me more words, I made new note cards. Then with each note card the students thought of more words they could add to the original word to come up with phrases. So for *next* they wrote things like *the next second* or *the next day* or *next year*.

Jessica then gave the students a few minutes to incorporate three sequence words into the story to help the reader understand the narrative flow.

Each day in class, Jessica introduced a similar process. The day after they worked on transitions, the class focused on action words. Again, the students returned to their stories and considered ways they could incorporate the new vocabulary to make the storytelling more vivid. After several days of revision, Jessica took the students' stories home, typed them, and wrote specific questions for the students when something seemed to be missing.

> In Flor's story, she had vultures planting poisonous mushrooms to kill the birds in Birdworld. But what wasn't clear was what the motivation was for the vultures to kill the birds. So I asked Flor, and many of the students, about the motivations of their characters. What were the reasons behind their actions? I also asked many of them why their character went back to the real world. Was it an accident or on purpose?

When Jessica returned to class, she met with each student individually. Rather than making suggestions, she asked questions that helped each person elaborate on her initial vision:

- What is the imaginary world like?
- Why does the destructive character want to destroy things?
- Why is the destruction a problem? Why does the main character want to stop the destructive character?
- What does the main character learn from going to the fantasy world?
- Why does the main character go back to the real world? By accident or on purpose?
- How does the character feel when she goes back to the real world? What does she change in the real world? How does she make it better?

As students answered, Jessica transcribed, capturing their exact language. She printed a transcript of their words and encouraged them to read the transcript, then return to their stories and add any new information they considered useful.

Discussing the project later, Jessica wisely noted, "I've learned not to tell kids just to add more. It doesn't work." Similarly, she explained that having students of this age give each other writing advice works sporadically at best. Jessica uses layering, not only across different mediums but also within the same medium, in this case writing. Each day she began class by introducing new words and encouraging the students to offer other words beyond the initial few she selected. The students then choose among the words to make phrases. These newly generated words and phrases provide the thick air the students needed to continue to revise their stories. The overall structure of the revision process was shaped by Jessica in close collaboration with the students.

SIMULTANEOUS WRITING AND ART MAKING

Karla, the teaching artist, joined Jessica's class as a guest artist, allowing Jessica time for writing conferences with her students. The previous year William Estrada, an artist from Chicago, visited Habla and taught the teachers how to use stop-motion animation as a medium for storytelling. Stop-motion animation is a filming technique in which artists combine a series of still photographs. In each photograph, the artist manipulates an object created out of any material—clay, cardboard, paper, or cloth—against a stationary backdrop. When the still photographs are sequenced one frame at a time, a story unfolds on the screen. Before digital movie-making, nearly all science fiction movies from *Godzilla* to *Star Wars* used stop-motion. Even today, many filmmakers use stop-motion to create a more tactile environment than digital imagery offers.

Using a simple computer program, a student can create a stop-motion animation film with only a digital camera. Karla, well versed in the technique, visited Jessica's class to help the students move from their storyboards to fully realized short films. She began by having the students read their stories and showing her their sketches as a prelude to painting the backgrounds of their two worlds on poster board.

While students worked on their settings, Jessica met with the students in the writing conferences described previously. The stop-motion animation project allowed Jessica to spend a generous amount of time in writing conferences, engaging each of her students in the revision process. Students returned from their conferences to edit their stories. Editing completed, they continued to paint their settings. Moving between writing and image-making helped the students to create more vivid versions of both. Flor, for instance, added specific objects and colors. Then she wrote, "I was transported to bird world. The first thing I saw was a very, very green forest and a blue river." The movement from medium to medium also provided the motivation to expand, enrich, and revise. Students found writing and editing their stories in a new language cognitively challenging and tiring. By moving from text to image, they recharged their cognitive batteries and approached their stories with a fresh perspective.

Image-making and writing continued simultaneously until the students completed the sets and revised their stories. Using construction paper, the students created and cut out the characters that inhabited their story worlds. As Karla worked with the students on the characters, Jessica moved the students in a new direction. At the beginning of class she said,

"Now you need to look at your stories to choose the lines that are absolutely essential for telling the story."

FRAMING: FINDING THE ESSENCE

Chicago teaching artist Cynthia Weiss refers to this process of reduction as *framing*. In her workshops, Cynthia hands her students frames of different sizes cut from black poster board. She explains that each of us sees only a small fraction of our total environment. By looking through frames, we further reduce our views and, at the same time, focus more clearly on what we see. Weiss invites students to wander around the room looking through the frames and experimenting with seeing from new perspectives. Students then make a framed image, share them with one another, and discuss what they find intriguing about what they see.

In another framing exercise, Cynthia instructs the students to write a description of their favorite place as a child, then to capture the essence of the place using only twenty-four words. After they read their twenty-four word descriptions, they reduce their descriptions to twelve words, then to six.

Often we think of revision as an additive process—more description, more details, more dialogue. Equally important is knowing what to delete. In a letter to Ernest Hemingway, F. Scott Fizgerald explained that for every page of writing he found acceptable, he threw ninety-nine pages in the trash.[14] Students work hard for their words on a page and don't want to throw any of it in the wastebasket. By setting clear and quantifiable limits, Cynthia forces students to frame their writing with a new lens. Similarly, after helping students to develop their stories, Jessica now asked them to reduce them to their essence. She explained, "We only have about one minute for each movie, so we'll time your reading it, and if it takes more than a minute, you'll need to take out more."

After editing, students gathered in a circle to read their stories aloud. Jessica worked with them on pronunciation, often asking the entire class to repeat a line or a word. After several rehearsals, the students recorded their stories on a digital recorder. If any were too long, Jessica sent them back to their desks for yet another revision. When Flor recorded her story, Jessica noted, "Flor surprised me. She didn't need me to pronounce the words for her. She knew how to say them. Her pronunciation was great, and she was very fluid." This was a stark contrast to earlier in the year when Flor could only speak a word or two, even when directly repeating the teacher's words.

As the recordings were being made, students worked in pairs to film the story. With characters positioned on the poster board setting, the author moved the characters and followed the story line. The other student held a camera about three feet off the ground and filmed, one exposure at a time. Although the process was painstakingly slow, the students worked with remarkable focus. Karla moved from pair to pair, coaching.

Habla doesn't have a computer lab where the students can download and organize their films using editing software like iMovie, but with the correct equipment, generally young people are quite skilled at editing images and sound to create their movies, with the more technologically savvy students coaching the others. In this project, Karla and Jessica edited photos and audio at home.

On the final day of the semester, students and their parents gathered in Habla's large performance and exhibit space. As the students' stories were projected, their recorded voices filled the room. Flor told her story.

One day I was in my house in Merida and I took my book of the birds of North America. I read the book under the bed and I was transported . . . to bird world. The first thing I saw was a very very green forest and blue river. I thought, "I like this world because it is big and cool." Later I made friends with the Tropic Bird, the Motmot, the Humming Bird, and the Grebe. We played a game to see who flies faster. We noticed that the gull ate mushrooms. But, there was a problem. The weird mushrooms cause sleep. The vultures planted the mushrooms because they want to kill the other birds. They wanted the bird world for themselves.

Suddenly there was a big problem. The vultures planted more weird mushrooms during the night. A lot of birds ate the mushrooms. The king of the birds was worried because the birds were inactive. I thought that we needed the help of the queen.

I flew to the castle to talk with the queen of the birds about the problem and look for one solution. The queen said that the vultures are cowards and weak. She suggested flying to the territory of vultures. The good birds (Tropic bird, Grebe, and Motmot) were furious because the vultures planted the mushrooms. There was a fight between the good birds and the vultures.

Next, I hit the bad vulture and the vultures ran. I won the gold medal because I was the hero of the birds. I flew and returned home to Merida so that my mom didn't search for me.

I learned that it's important to save the birds so that they have a place to live and don't get extinct. In Merida, I save all the birds.

UNCOVERING LANGUAGE

After the performance, we asked Karla and Jessica what they thought contributed most to Flor's language development. In a year, Flor had moved from being nearly silent in class and writing only individual words to expressing herself clearly, speaking and writing in a new language.

Her teachers noted that she first came into class with a large vocabulary in Spanish. Karla explained, "When I first met her, I noticed she had an elevated vocabulary in Spanish. She knew many words that other students didn't know, especially the scientific names of animals. But she only spoke with one word or two. If we talked about an animal, she called out the scientific name. But no more." Jessica said that Flor could call up specific words but had difficulty expressing herself in full sentences. "Flor got stuck when it was time to start writing words. She'd have the story inside of her in Spanish, but she could only express herself with individual words. She had words, some in English and some in Spanish, but couldn't put them together."

Both teachers thought that the classroom community contributed the most to Flor's language development. Jessica explained,

I think her classmates had the most to do with her growth. We definitely had a space in the classroom where everyone participated, encouraged each other, and worked together. Flor is very creative. A lot of the things we worked on were very creative. Flor thinks in a different sort of way. So when we did human sculptures, Flor would think of a different way to do a human sculpture than anybody else, and her classmates recognized that and her classmates grew from that. It was a good environment for learning together.

As mentioned earlier, Karla indicated that she noted Flor becoming more engaged in the classroom the week when the class made Flor's birds central to their weekly performance.

The first step in Flor's growth resulted from the presence of a supportive classroom community, one where Flor felt valued by her teachers and classmates. Karla contrasted Flor's experience at Habla with Flor's more traditional schooling.

After the first summer Flor was really excited about coming back to Habla, even though she at first had trouble opening up with a new teacher. When I talked to Flor, she remembered specific things we made that first summer. She was saying, "Remember when we made the self-portraits." It was a good change for her. I think the school where she is now she is not accepted; she has never been accepted. Here she was totally accepted. That was a big difference for her. That is why returning here was important to her.

Jessica echoed these sentiments.

I don't know much about the school she goes to but often at the beginning of our class she would say, "Oh, school was terrible or I failed this exam or the teacher yelled at us or we had to be quiet all day long." She indicates in a lot of different ways that she's not very happy at her school or maybe not valued at her school. I think that Flor has a lot inside her. I think from the very beginning she had a lot of vocabulary and she brought with her a lot of language abilities that just hadn't been uncovered and that she hadn't had a space to let them grow.

Flor's teachers identify her sense of being valued and accepted as a significant factor in her language development, what we referred to previously as feeling a sense of belonging. Language theorist Stephen Krashen coined the term *affective filter* to indicate the emotional barrier that prevents language learning.[15] At the outset, Flor refused, consciously or subconsciously, to take the risks necessary to practice, develop, and refine her English. By directly honoring Flor's talents and passions—her birds—her teachers created space for those talents to flourish in a language-learning context.

Yet Jessica and Karla not only allowed Flor to pursue her passion for sketching birds in the classroom, but they also designed a layered process involving multiple steps in different symbol systems that let Flor put her talents as an artist and her interest in birds to work to *uncover* her language abilities. The moves Jessica and Karla made involved several opportunities for Flor to translate across—and revise within—mediums:

- Read *The Lorax*
- Map the structure of the story
- Discuss the plot, setting, and characters
- Sketch imaginary and real worlds and characters
- Translate words to describe the worlds and characters
- Present the worlds and characters to the class and tell outlines of the stories
- Plan the structure of the story
- Draw the story on storyboards
- Translate from images to words and then again from Spanish to English
- Tell the story several times during the story walks
- Expand and rewrite stories adding new ideas
- Design and paint the settings of the stories
- Revise stories adding new words
- Create the characters for the animations
- Synthesize stories to their essence
- Practice reading stories to achieve fluency

- Photograph stop-motion animations
- Perform stories into a recorder
- Edit stop-motion animations (if technology is available)
- Present stop-motion animations for an audience

When an experience has multiple layers, students engage in deliberate practice because of the generous amount of time allowed for the experience. In such a complex project, when something goes wrong, when a student writes a description she isn't satisfied with or draws a character that doesn't meet her expectations, because the project is extended over a period of time, she has time to rewrite a section of her story, paint a new setting, or refilm or reedit her animation. Important as deadlines are, the real world rarely asks us to complete assignments and turn them in to be assessed every day. The work of the real world involves complex and iterative processes: putting together a business plan, preparing for a trial, managing the healing of a patient, writing a magazine article, or designing and teaching a course—rarely linear processes. They involve conversations, research, reflection, writing, and multiple experiments with technology. We often need to work through difficulties to achieve the desired result. Complex processes allow us to bring our skills and talents to the task. We learn new things because they assist us in reaching our goals.

In this and other large projects that Karla and Jessica introduced in their classrooms, Flor found a home for her birds. Earlier in the year, Jessica taught a unit around a Native American myth, "How Stories Came to Be." The students wrote their versions of how stories came into the world. In Flor's story, a magpie visits a boy every night to tell him the very first stories. In all her stories, birds play a divine role.

Currently, Karla is working with Flor outside of school on a much larger project. Flor is visiting ecological parks in the Yucatan. With the help of professional biologists, photographers, and artists, she is drawing the illustrations for a field guide to the birds of the Yucatan. She has been working on this project with Karla and the other adults for two years, and as of this writing, the project still hasn't been completed. Karla explained,

I can say this about Flor: she is now an expert. It's not just about the two of us working together, but her working with the biologist and the photographer. She can now take advantage of all the benefits of this project. She knows that it takes time, a lot of time to complete something, but that it is worth it. It has taken us more than two years to work on this and we don't have anything completed. We have the illustrations, some of the information, but when we put it together something is missing. All these years working on the project has opened her eyes. She says, "I don't want to leave it like this. I want it to be more." Right now we don't know where the project is going. But I know that she knows, and one day she will tell us how to help her complete it. We are only giving her some tools. She's learning in different levels, not just learning a language, not just about birds, but about many things, learning how to research, even learning how to live life.

Revision takes time and can prove difficult. But when we care about making our work better, we put in the time and make the necessary effort. The kind of stamina and persistence required to complete a complex project is one of the most difficult skills to teach. Perhaps it can't be taught. Perhaps it can only be experienced.

FOR THE CLASSROOM

REHEARSING—FOR THE CLASSROOM

Thematic Stories

In this chapter we describe how students wrote their own imaginative stories based on Dr. Seuss's *The Lorax*. A similar process for writing and performing stories using storyboards was developed for secondary students at Brown Summer High School by educator Len Newman and theater artist Fred Sullivan. Len and Fred were teaching Shakespeare's *Othello*, and their students performed their own stories based on themes they drew from the play.

Len began the story-writing process by telling a story from his own life. The story the teacher selects will help set the tone of the stories students will tell. Len always tells a story that is particularly close to his heart. If students realize the teacher is opening his life to them, they are more likely to tell deeper stories rather than the stereotypical "breaking arm" or "visiting Six Flags" stories.

After telling his story, Len asks his students to begin thinking about their own stories that relate to the text they are reading in class. Handing out paper, he asks them to write a title, sentence, or image that captures the story. (For more ways to help students find ideas for their writing, see the brainstorming activities in chapter 5.) Len then instructs the students to take a piece of paper and fold it horizontally into three even sections.

In each section, the students draw pictures or write sentences representing the beginning, middle, and end of their stories. In pairs, using the simple structure of the three-part storyboard, students then tell their stories to each other.

Once the students share their stories, they turn their papers over and fold them lengthwise to create six spaces. In these six spaces the students elaborate on their initial drawings and sentences, creating two images or sentences each for their stories' beginning, middle, and end.

Fred Sullivan, the actor and director, then places the students in groups of four or five. After listening to everyone's stories, each group chooses one story to dramatize. The selected student then tells her story again to the group, and the group creates a rough improvisation to bring to the "stage" in about twenty minutes. At the end of class the groups performs their stories for each other. Fred repeats this performance process over the course of four or five days so that each student's story is performed. Fred and the class discuss what worked in each performance. He then gives the overall class "director's notes," or ideas from the theater that they might consider as they create additional performances.

Students also write a narrative version of their stories that incorporates dialogue from the improvised scenes. Fred and Len lead discussions in which the students compare and contrast their original stories with the story and characters in *Othello*.

For the culminating performance, each group chooses one story to perform for the community. The class also might create a book of all the class stories and each student receives a copy.

Following is a summary of Fred and Len's writing and performing process:

1. Write or draw initial idea.
2. Write or draw B, M, E.
3. Tell story in pairs.
4. Write or draw BB, MM, EE.
5. Tell stories in group.
6. Select one story to improvise.
7. Rehearse and perform one story a day.
8. Reflect on each performance.
9. Repeat for all stories.
10. Students individually write and revise stories at home and in class.
11. Groups choose one story for final performance.
12. Rehearse and perform final story.

13. Edit and publish all stories in a class book.

Editing on Your Feet

Jan Mandell originally introduced the process of editing on your feet to us at Brown Summer High School.

The class moves to an open space where there is plenty of room to walk. Students line up on one side of the space standing shoulder-to-shoulder. The students walk to the other side of the room and back telling their stories out loud but not speaking to anyone in particular. They need to time their storytelling so that they finish telling their stories by the time they return to their places.

Once they return, give them a new lens through which to view their stories. You might explain, "Now emotions. What did you feel? What was going on inside your heart? What are all the different conflicting emotions? Tell the story from that perspective." If the stories are fictional or about other people, you might ask, "What does your protagonist feel? What is going on inside her heart?" Students walk again.

When they return again offer another prompt. For example, "Now when you walk you're going to try to remember location and the little details about the place. Where were you? What did it look like? How did it smell? What were the different colors? What kind of day was it?"

You may continue this process through several different iterations with a different prompt for each telling. Finally say, "Now I'm going to ask you to put all those things together as you tell your story."

Using Cynthia Weiss's idea of framing, you may ask students to condense the stories, helping them find the essence. Explain that this time they must finish telling their entire story before reaching the other side of the room, "Now you're going to focus on the beginning, the middle, and the end, and you're going to condense your story. By the time you get to the other side of the room, you'll need to end the story. You're going to have to condense it, much like playwriting, because playwrights don't tell every single thing that's going on in someone's life. They condense the play to just the essential things. So what are the essential moments in your story?"

For the final story revision explain, "This last time you're going to tell your story as you walk just halfway across the room. So you're going to shorten it, reducing it to its essence. Don't think too hard; just find a beginning, middle and end, and go."

Next, students pair up to tell their stories to each other in thirty seconds. The leader keeps mixing the pairs so that students have the chance to tell their stories many times and hear the other stories in the classroom. After the students have had ample time to edit on their feet, they revise them using all the ideas they developed during the process.

7

Performing Text

"Now I Am Here Telling My Story"

The aesthetic space possesses . . . properties which stimulate knowledge and discovery, cognition and recognition: properties which stimulate the process of learning by experience.

—AUGUSTO BOAL

I learned this, at least, by my experiment: that if one advances confidently in the direction of his dreams, and endeavors to live the life which he has imagined, he will meet with a success unexpected in common hours.

—HENRY DAVID THOREAU

IT WAS A SWELTERING DAY in the Central Falls High School auditorium. The blue-velvet stage curtain separated the backstage from the classes streaming into their seats. Seven hundred students already counting down the remaining days to summer break tested their teachers' limits. A cup flew from the seats to the stage, soaking the wooden floor with Dunkin' Donuts iced coffee, an act that reflected the tone of the previous few school days.

Meanwhile, behind the curtain Len Newman and Richard Kinslow's students, many of whom had been in the United States for less than a year, stood in a circle. Their teachers led them through preperformance warm-ups. "Shake down countdown," Len called out, extending his arm and shaking it. "5. 4. 3. 2. 1." The students laughed and followed him as he shook his other arm, legs, then his whole body spasmodically. As the auditorium filled with the restless, energetic audience, Len took the performers' minds off their nerves, focusing instead on their customary warm-up rituals. Just before the show began, Richard gathered the students in a circle and asked for quiet. Then he spoke to them.

> For three months you've been telling each other your stories. Your stories of coming here to the United States. The stories of your dreams for the future. Now is the time to share these stories with your parents, with your friends, and with your teachers. This is your performance. This is your gift. Hands in the middle. A big "Dream Keepers" and go to your opening places. *Dream Keepers!*

Hearing the call, the raucous auditorium quieted. Len and Richard stepped in front of the curtain to welcome everyone to the performance. "These are the Dream Keepers, and these are their stories . . ."

DREAM KEEPERS IN AN URBAN HIGH SCHOOL

The old mill city of Central Falls, Rhode Island, covers one square mile. Per capita, it holds the largest immigrant population in the state and one of the largest in New England. Many families are originally from Puerto

Rico, the Dominican Republic, Guatemala, Colombia, Mexico, Brazil, Haiti, and Cape Verde. The cultural resources of this community—and therefore of its schools—are astounding. Multiple cultures share languages, dances, music, and food. But the Central Falls School District also reports a dropout rate of 48 percent and the densest, most economically disadvantaged population in Rhode Island. The city has the state's greatest percentage of children under the age of six living in poverty. Most recently, it has gained considerable notoriety as a school that, in its attempt to "reform," fired and then rehired all its teachers.[1]

In the years that the ArtsLiteracy Project collaborated with a group of teachers and students in Central Falls, we encountered many hard-working, dedicated teachers. Richard Kinslow and Len Newman's pioneering Newcomers class ranked as perhaps the most diverse classroom in the district. Their students had recently arrived in the United States with little or no English and often little literacy in their home language as well. The performance *We Are the Dream Keepers: These Are Our Stories* was the culmination of an extended unit of study Kinslow and Newman designed to introduce these students to the school and the community.

STANDING FIRM AND TALL

The curtain opened in the overheated auditorium. Santiago Medina lay on stage facing the audience, pretending to be asleep.[2] His recorded voice boomed through the large speakers.

> On Thursday, January 23, 2003, I left my country, El Salvador, for the United States of America. On the twenty-second, I said goodbye to all of my family, and at four o'clock the next morning I took the bus from my home to the capital city where I arrived at nine o'clock, a little hungry because I had not eaten anything.

Although he had been speaking English for only a little more than a year, Santiago sounded strong and confident. Larger-than-life puppets representing both his memories and his dreams for the future floated across the stage behind him as he told his story. Santiago's recorded narrative included the story of two days spent hidden beneath the seat of a car and the experience of being held at gunpoint by robbers. He recounted the journey that had brought him to the United States and, finally, onto a plane bound for Providence to reunite with his mother.

> It was night, and I was very tired from the long ride. I hadn't seen my mother in twelve years, since I was four years old. I had only seen her in photos. I did not know if I would recognize her, but I was happy because I was in the United States and because I would soon be with my mother again. My mother saw me, and she knew me right away. She had brought a picture of me, and now I am here telling my story.

Large, brilliantly painted portraits of the mother and son emerged from opposite sides of the stage, met in the middle, and embraced as fully as cardboard cutouts can.

When the performance ended and Santiago and his fellow students had told their stories, each one illustrated by life-size puppets, their teacher, Richard, said of his class's performance process:

> Great stories were not only heard by a rapt audience during the final performance, but also in the weeks before as we listened in the sanctity of our own classroom. As students wrote their stories, we shared them every day. When we told the stories in class, we were mesmerized. You could have heard the proverbial pin drop. During the final performance, the students came onto the stage standing firm and tall.[3]

If we had to set one standard for all schools across the United States, perhaps it would be for students to graduate "standing firm and tall." The New London Group writes that "literacy educators and students must see themselves as active participants in social change, as learners and students who can be active designers—makers—of social futures."[4] The students in Richard and Len's class demonstrated who they were and what they had learned to do, not only with the English language but with all of their creative talents on display for the community. They offered their audience windows into their worlds, both in their home countries and in the United States. During the performance, the school's principal turned to one of the teachers and commented, "I didn't know *these students* could do this." Suddenly, "these students," new to the school and the United States and with limited English proficiency, stood in front of their community telling their stories. Answering audience questions with confidence after the show, they challenged others' assumptions of who they were and what they could do, demonstrating that they could indeed play an active role in shaping their futures.

MEANINGFUL PLAY

Richard and Len's students needed to learn a set of linguistic and cognitive skills for success in mainstream English classes. The teachers' approaches to helping them gain these skills focused—first and foremost—on inspiring them to *want* to do extensive reading and writing in and out of school. Although there was a consistent and explicit focus on learning vocabulary, applying strategies, and using correct grammatical structures, the teachers sought first and foremost to help students understand the purpose of the work and its connection with their lived experience as young persons with rich opportunities and promising futures.

To reach this goal, students viewed and created written and spoken texts and visual art designed to culminate in a final performance. With their teachers, they visited area museums to experience and discuss art. In the classroom, the students listened to music of performers such as Miles Davis and learned about his life as an artist. They read a range of primary sources and literature about people traveling across physical and metaphorical borders, including the poetry of Langston Hughes, short stories and essays by Sandra Cisneros and Edwidge Danticat, and myths from *Ovid*, including Icarus and Daedalus. The teachers wanted students to interact with the material, experiment, and play using the many literacies—or *multiliteracies*—at their disposal.

Applied to education, the word *play* has unfortunately come to imply superficiality and the teaching approach Lucy Calkins disparagingly calls "literature based arts and crafts."[5] In such coursework, students might examine a book for a few days and then take part in an "arts" activity by creating a poster presentation or diorama that does not deepen the discussion of the text or further the class's learning objectives. In contrast, what we call *meaningful play* in the classroom setting fosters significant learning in and through the arts. The students in the Newcomers class engaged with literature and art in order to enter into conversations with these texts, to reflect on their own lives, to develop their own stories

In defining characteristics of art, neuroscientist Merlin Donald writes that "the artistic object compels reflection on the very process that created it . . . Art is thus inherently metacognitive in its cognitive function on both the individual and social levels."[6] When they engaged with literature, music, and visual art, Len and Richard's students considered how these works developed, how they reflected the world of the artists, and how they might create their own works to reflect their identities and dreams. To introduce meaningful play in the classroom, Len and Richard invited Erminio Pinque, the artistic director of a renowned performance troupe of visual artists, performers, and musicians called Big Nazo, based in nearby Providence, to work with the class to create a performance that would tell the stories of their dreams using larger-than-life-size cardboard puppets. In an e-mail to Len Newman, Erminio commented:

> I think your idea of exposing the students to the work of the Surrealists like Dali and Chagall is a great one. Exposure to expressionism and Dadaism would also be helpful in providing examples of how non-linear thinking, memory-collage and the creation of seemingly "non-sense" images can serve to define and manifest the subject matter and inner life of the subconscious.[7]

In planning the Newcomers curriculum, the teachers explicitly considered how key works of art might help the students find the words and images to narrate their own lives and stories. The opportunity to play with art, as viewers and creators, invites learners to develop and use higher-level cognitive processes. Involvement in the arts calls for "enactment of role-playing" and "sustained visual focus," critical tools for language development.[8] To move toward their class's goals for language learning, Richard and Len therefore turned away from language drills and "arts and crafts" curriculum to introduce meaningful play with arts.

PERFORMANCE EVERY DAY

Every day in the Newcomers class, students not only learned through various art forms but also, crucially, read and performed texts in English, their second language. The students came to the class with very little exposure to English and were starting at a basic level. Often, beginning language classes start with a grammatical approach, focusing on sound-symbol relationships and structure before meaning. In this classroom students simultaneously worked on the development of fluency, vocabulary, *and* substantive readings of literary texts. The Newcomers class did not withhold literature pending the mastery of basic English grammar. Instead, literature—as an art form that students could interpret—provided a foundation and a purpose for learning the language from the very beginning.

Len Newman described their approach:

We read *every* day. We promoted oral language activities *every* day. We sang *every* day. We had a performance piece almost every day. This came about seven years into playing with arts integration. In the first few years, I might do a unit that might last twenty school days and might do a performance piece or two from time to time. By the time I got to this point, the fabric was to integrate the arts completely with text. Every encounter with text has an artistic aspect connected to it whether it is visual art, performance, or movement. We were able to structure the class in such a way that the focus of the class was for full integration every day, and kids read and wrote every day.[9]

Students did not shift categorically from *text* to *art*. In this classroom, various art forms informed and built on one another, serving as a central means of representing and communicating their work. Arts integration, as Len learned, meant moving back and forth each class period from reading to performing in order to establish an ever-deepening understanding and engagement with language. In chapter 6 we refer to layering experiences as a means of achieving a greater depth of understanding by moving among artistic and textual mediums. Similarly, Len and Richard tied each arts experience directly to a portion of a print text students had in hand. They discussed, for example, what a line like "dry up like a raisin in the sun" could mean as they collaboratively interpreted the line in movement. Text informed every experience and, as Len Newman noted with emphasis, the students read *every* day. In class, the conversation did not center on grades. Instead, everyone read, wrote, made art, and performed.

Connecting arts experiences directly to texts deepened the students' understanding of English. During the year, they used the words they were reading and writing to create small daily performances for one another. Later, the teachers collected and published their written and illustrated stories in a book they named *Stories Keep Our Cultures Alive* and gave each student a copy to take home. At year's end, the students' *Dream Keepers* performance showcased their learning and language growth for their fellow students and for the community at large.

AN AESTHETIC EVENT

Storytelling provides the foundation of literacy in all cultures. In his novels and stories, Gabriel García Márquez recaptures the magical tales he heard his grandparents tell. Homer recounted epic poems passed from generation to generation. Around a contemporary dinner table, the conversation moves from story to story, from an account of a common event from someone's day, to a joke, to a retelling of a movie or a television episode. With today's pervasive digital technology, many of us create and share stories through personalized Web sites and other social media platforms.

Finding words for our experiences is a performative act that allows us to shape our identity and share it with the wider world. Paulo Freire points to this connection between word and world as critical for literacy development. The creative and aesthetic act of attaching images to words enriches reading and writing. Explaining his own literacy development, Freire writes, "I had such an almost physical connection with the text. It was this experience that began to teach me how reading is also an act of beauty because it has to do with the reader rewriting the text. It's an aesthetical event."[10] For Freire, reading became an artistic creation. As he read and formed his own interpretations, he was "rewriting the text." Reading, we might then say, is *inherently* performative; to be understood, words must be enacted in the inner world of the mind.

When children see themselves as active participants in this cognitive performance, they not only become literate but also learn to love the act of reading. The magic of this aesthetic event represents what educator Emilia Ferreiro identifies as the key feature that draws some children into a life of reading: "There are children who enter written language through magic (a cognitively challenging magic) and other children who enter written language through training in 'basic abilities.' In general, the first become readers; the others have an uncertain fate."[11] Ferreiro's "magic" does not simply appear. It begins with the assistance of others and subsequently requires a "cognitively challenging" effort. For students to become insightful and reflective readers, they must delve deeply into text, wrestle with meaning, and feel these meanings resonate within themselves. Teachers can inspire language learners to embark on a life in which print text plays a significant role. In Richard and Len's class, meaningful, artful play allowed students access to this magic.

THE STORIES THAT BEG TO BE PERFORMED

By late March, the Newcomers class had spent several weeks exploring the sometimes concrete, sometimes abstract world of dreams. Richard described the experience of hearing his students tell their stories: "It was a springboard effect. One student after another told of their experience of coming to America. It went right around the room. These are kids you typically can't get to write anything in class. Santiago went right home and wrote five pages."

Telling their stories to a classroom audience proved incredibly powerful for these language learners. As Len explained, "They told stories of the life back in their home country, the people they left behind, and the perils they encountered on their way to a new land. These are the stories that they have been waiting to have someone ask them to tell. These are the stories that beg to be written and eventually performed." Often, telling their own stories proved emotionally difficult, but the students pushed on, eager to express themselves and be heard. As Richard recalled,

> One of the kids told a story on Friday about the night his mother died in Guatemala. As he got toward the end, he broke down, which is understandable. But this sobbing boy felt he had to tell this story, and as he gathered himself, the silent respect of his community of rapt listeners was as poignant as anything that you'll ever experience as a teacher or a student in a classroom. It takes great courage to do that kind of work, and it takes great risk to demonstrate that kind of courage.

After finding their stories, the students moved to performing them. Erminio Pinque returned to the class, this time with a minidisc recorder, a microphone, and an amplifier. He took students aside one by one and asked them questions about their lives. Most students told of the journey from their home country to the United States. Erminio prompted students with questions and recorded their responses. Sometimes he helped with usage or pronunciation. When the student made a mistake, Erminio simply rerecorded.

Once he finished recording each student, Erminio played the recordings for the whole class. Students beamed upon hearing their own voices, rich and loud, recounting their stories in fluent English. The class applauded each performance enthusiastically. The students then drew self-portraits. Erminio projected the self-portraits onto six-foot pieces of cardboard, and the students created life-size puppets. The puppets, combined with the recorded soundtrack, provided the basis for the performance. By deciding to prerecord the lines for the show, Erminio, Len, and Richard gave students the opportunity to hear their own voices in fluent English, offering them dignity, a sense of pride, and a concrete model of the linguistic excellence they can achieve on their own. Hearing their own voices made the goal seem more attainable and personal.

BECOMING VISIBLE

Performing in school gives students the opportunity to become participants rather than spectators. By its very nature, performance has the potential to change the dynamics of the teaching environment. As Lisa Delpit explains, "The teacher can't be the only expert in the room. To deny students their own expert knowledge is to disempower them."[12] For performance to be empowering, teachers and students must become collaborators in the performance process. Over the years we've witnessed many performances in schools in which students read lines they don't fully understand or go through the physical act of performing without a sense that the role has any real personal meaning for them. In contrast, the teachers and artists involved in the "Dream Keepers" unit approached performance as an opportunity for their students to craft and share narratives of their lives with the larger community. As Richard stated, "I don't care that much about the final performance. That belongs to them. They'll do it, and it will be great." The teachers and the artists were there to offer advice, suggest possibilities, and help structure the overall work. But the students wrote the stories, decided on the stage movements, and constructed life-size puppets. When teachers trust the students to make these decisions, the students own the performance.

In work like the "Dream Keepers" unit, students create performances that tell their own stories. In others such as the *Song of Myself* performance described in chapter 5, students link their own stories to notable, challenging texts. In either case, if done well, the gains are powerful. Students expand their own understanding and worldview by considering what they must do to present words and ideas—whether their own or Whitman's—to others. Having done so, expectations change concerning what "those kids" can achieve. A student who struggles with test taking might be able to think, write, and speak beautifully. The audience will see that student differently the moment she steps onstage with confidence and begins,

> I CELEBRATE myself, and sing myself
> And what I assume you shall assume
> For every atom belonging to me as good belongs to you.

If we believe in the power of public education to educate all students, then we must believe in finding ways to make all of them visible in schools.

LEARNING IN THE MOMENT

Many activities in school function as dry runs for something that will happen later in life. Oftentimes, students lose sight of the purpose of these activities and become disengaged from their own learning. As David Perkins notes,

> Most educational practice reflects what might be called an *export paradigm*. What learners do today focuses on exporting knowledge for use in a range of envisioned futures. The math in the textbook is for application somewhere, sometime, in some supermarket or on some income tax form or during possible careers in business, engineering, or science . . . The specific activities—problem sets for honing skills, answering questions toward understanding principles, memorizing information toward quizzes—are blatantly exercises that target much later payoffs.[13]

Unfortunately, for many students the recommendation that they work hard in the present to achieve a long-term payoff is not convincing. The steps they need to take between their present circumstances and promised futures are unclear, the path too inaccessible or unappealing. The rote tasks and endless dry runs in a subject area seem pointless. Learning to read, for example, often includes twelve years of interpretive exercises, chasing hidden meanings the teacher understands but they do not, memorizing unfamiliar words they can never imagine using, defining terms like *metaphor* and *protagonist,* and answering comprehension questions at the end of chapters—all activities supposedly intended to prepare for college and adult life. Overemphasizing the long-term payoff diminishes their immediate experience. Certainly we need to encourage students to work hard to build a body of knowledge for the future, yet we also want them to feel confident, smart, and capable. We want them to be able to contribute to their community in the present moment.

When students perform, they contribute to their immediate worlds. They feel the energy between themselves and their audiences. Acknowledging its power, many educators incorporate different forms of performance into curriculum. Ted Sizer, for example, wrote extensively about the value of students demonstrating their learning in what he called *exhibitions* and others call *performances of understanding.*[14]

We strive for moments of this sort, when all aspects of the Performance Cycle culminate in products or events students can show to others. At these moments, young people stand before an audience of peers or communities, confident in their own voices, their own words, and the words of their people. At these moments, they feel safe in their classrooms and school communities. They have been inspired to interpret art and texts from multiple cultures and from various times. They summon the courage to risk public presentations. Their learning is legitimized.

In the *Dream Keepers* performance, Santiago's recorded voice ended and the real Santiago stood up. He had spoken his own words, written in response to all of the great authors he had studied—Hughes, Danticat, and Cisneros. He had shared his words with his classmates throughout the year. Twenty-five of his peers stood beside him, all having told their stories. He spoke to the audience: "I told this story because I remember everything that happened to me. I told it because I have a new life now. My name is Santiago Medina. I am sixteen years old." The audience stood and cheered. Smiling broadly, each of the students took a final bow.

FOR THE CLASSROOM

PERFORMING TEXT

Since performances are exhibitions of individual and collective learning, you may want to view them as a living portfolio of a student's work. Arts-Literacy performances are more like a *bricolage* of different elements, all brought together under a central concept or theme. In the Creating Text chapter, the guiding concept was "A Song of Myself," and the performances combined segments of Whitman's poetry alongside the student's original "songs" as told through different artistic mediums: dance, photography, music, and poetry readings. In the Entering Text and Comprehending Text chapters, the central concept was inheritance. The students performed scenes from *The Piano Lesson*, created montages from *The House on Mango Street*, read monologues from *The Joy Luck Club*, and presented their own original poetry on stage.

Performances are organized around individual, small-group, and whole-class pieces. We often create performances of about twenty minutes using the following structure:

- Entire group opening
- Individual
- Small group
- Individual
- Small group
- Individual
- Small group

- Individual
- Small group
- Individual
- Small group
- Individual
- Entire group closing

Classrooms are divided into five small groups, and each group creates and directs its own piece of the performance. All groups and individuals share their work in the classroom with their peers. When presenting to the larger community, we often ask for individual volunteers. Of course, we have deviated from the above structure in numerous ways, but this general organizing idea has persisted through hundreds of performances over twelve years.

Nearly every activity presented in earlier "For the Classroom" sections can be easily presented in a performance. For instance, Kurt was leading a weeklong teacher institute with a group of elementary teachers in Chicago in collaboration with Chicago Partnerships in Arts Education. Early in the week, the teachers participated in a variety of performance activities, including Mirroring (see chapter 2) and Rapid Tableaus (see chapter 3). Normally these activities might be viewed as only a part of the process. At the end of the week, instead of creating a culminating performance from scratch, they presented the activities on stage, illustrating them as a part of the learning process. The performance then organically grew out of the experiences of the week.

Similarly, in Len Newman and Richard Kinslow's classroom described in this chapter, Erminio Pinque, the performance artist, taught the students how to manipulate their puppets in a way that clearly told a story. In preparing for the performance, Erminio simply encouraged the students to do what they had been doing throughout the entire semester: enjoy themselves while using their puppets to tell a story. The students had created all the rough pieces for the performance by improvising around each of their classmates' stories. Preparing for their performance, they simply replicated what they had been doing all along in rehearsal.

Nearly all approaches listed below can be performed individually, in small groups, or as an entire class, with some slight adjustments. Take Lady Macbeth's monologue in *Macbeth*. One student can perform it on stage. But you may also give a group of five or six students the monologue and ask them to find a way to perform it collectively. Or perhaps each student in the class takes a line from it and steps forward and presents it as the rest of the class moves in the background in the Human Atom formation (see chapter 2).

The class can invent performance approaches for taking the collective work of the semester and bringing it to the stage. We offer here only a few possibilities for designing performances and inspiring conversation among teachers and students.

Monologues

Ask for volunteers to commit a portion of a text to memory and present it during the performance as a monologue. If teaching a theater text, an actual monologue can be presented. We often pair monologues from a core text with the original work of the students. For instance, at Central Falls High School, an English language learners' class was reading *Othello*. The students wrote and performed their own stories about jealousy. To open the performance, a student presented Othello's closing monologue in which he admits to being a person who "loved not wisely, but too well," setting the context for the rest of the performance. Between the ensemble presentations of the student's original stories, individual students took the stage and read short monologues about jealousy from the various characters in Shakespeare's play.

Poetry Readings and Storytelling

Another option is to have groups perform scenes from the core text. If the students are reading *To Kill a Mockingbird*, they might stage various versions of the trial scene. During the year they can write their own poetry or stories that relate to the themes of *To Kill a Mockingbird* and create a performance in which individual students read their poetry or stories between the scenes from the core text.

Silent Storytelling

Each group of students has about two or three pages of text to read and perform. This performance approach often works best when each section of text has clear developing action.

The group first needs to spend time reading the text together and figuring out what the six big actions of the scene are. The group will then bring the scene to performance based on agreed-on guidelines:

- Perform the scene only with physical movement; no words or props are allowed

- Focus on clearly telling the story so a person in the audience who has never read it will understand who the characters are and what they are doing in the scene
- Keep the tone of the original text; avoid making a serious text a comedy

Music adds an additional layer to the performances. Each group can determine the kind of music they would like to use in their scene based on the instruments and talents that are available in the classroom. It often works well to have a member from another group play the musical accompaniment to the scene. We've experienced quite powerful scenes when a drum, flute, or guitar supports the movement on the stage.

Slide Show Tableaus

In groups, students select six big events from the central text that they consider important in conveying its core meaning. Each group creates six tableaus, each communicating the essence of that moment in the story. Encourage students to select moments that are active and where there is dramatic tension between characters. The group may then write a narrative to accompany the tableaus. Students then perform the series of tableaus accompanied by the narration.

Bricolage

Students work through multiple artistic mediums, separate from each other, and then bring these different mediums together to create a *bricolage*. An important aspect of bricolage is the idea of student choice. Students have the opportunity to create an artistic work in a medium they feel comfortable with.

1. Choose a small portion of text to guide the activity. The text should have either stark images that lend themselves to visual work or a clear line of action that might inspire movement or theater work.
2. Select the mediums students will have the opportunity to work in and invite individual students in the class to choose their medium.

3. Based on their choices, organize students into small groups. Each group has time to interpret the text through their chosen artistic medium.

4. In a larger performance, combine all mediums. For instance, one group of students might create a dance/movement piece based on the text. Another group uses the text as a springboard for poetry. Two other groups choose to create visual art that captures the text's essence. For the performance, the visual art is projected onto a screen in the form of digital slides, while the movement group performs in front of the screen. The poetry group reads their poetry during the movement piece. The final performance is then a simultaneous realization of movement, visual art, and poetry.

Through bricolage, a new artistic work will emerge that is a collaborative effort of the entire class. By combining artistic mediums, each art form is simultaneously transformed.

Character Journeys

Character Journeys is an approach that can be used either before, during, or after students read a text. As a group, students select lines from a character and present the journey of the character throughout a chapter, scene, or book by creating a tableau with words.

If this approach is used after the students have read a text, give each group of students a different focal character. For instance, after reading *The Great Gatsby*, one group will focus on Gatsby, another on Daisy, another on Tom, etc. In their groups the students identify lines that show the character's journey throughout the novel. After collecting all the lines, the group then decides on the most essential lines—one for each person in the group.

Each person memorizes his line. Students may simply present their lines with an accompanying gesture. A more dynamic way is for one student to enter the stage, read her line, and form a frozen sculpture. The second student enters, reads his line, and adds to the sculpture. This continues as each member of the group enters and adds themselves to the sculpture. When everyone from the group is on stage and frozen, the group calls out their character's name and exits the stage.

Layered Performances

This idea for layered performances is inspired by the theory of layering presented in chapter 6. We found that when we asked students to create performances with no boundaries, the performances felt more like skits that lacked the commitment and aesthetic we were looking for. For instance, the students might become focused on designing props and lose their focus on truly bringing the text to life on the stage in a way that captures the essential elements of the story.

To begin, divide the class into small performance groups. Give each group a portion of text to bring to performance. Explain that each group will have about twenty minutes to read the text and come to a shared understanding of it and bring the text to the stage. In all of the following layers, explain that the students must communicate the tone of the original text.

- *Layer One.* For the first layer the students bring the text to the stage only using their voices. As a group they will figure out how to present the text vocally (see "Choral Reading" in chapter 4). They make a conscious decision about their physical placement as they perform. After the groups perform for one another, add the second layer to the performances.
- *Layer Two.* Now the groups add minimal movement to their pieces. They figure out how they will enter and exit the stage and how they will move during the performance.

Variation

Another example of a layered performance is based on Silent Storytelling.

- *Layer One.* Give the students a core text and have them develop three silent tableaus that clearly communicate the story. Perform for the rest of the group.

- *Layer Two.* Now the students add movement. They may choose now to use the tableaus or omit them. The focus as always should be clearly communicating the story of the text.
- *Layer Three.* Offer the students a variety of instruments. They may now add musical accompaniment that enhance the power of the physical movement but only with one student playing one instrument. They will need to adjust their movement piece, since one student will either be in the piece playing the instrument or off to the side playing for the rest of the ensemble.
- *Layer Four.* Pair each small group with another small group. One group will be the musical ensemble for the other group. The students in one group can choose a variety of instruments that help communicate the tone of their partner group's movement piece.

As the layering process continues, choose what you would like the students to add to their overall performance. You might provide a box of costumes or props or material for the students to make their own. The key is that by developing the performance incrementally, the students can learn from the other students' performances, make adjustments along the way, and slowly develop the quality of their work. Likewise, the teacher can monitor how the groups are developing and offer feedback or vary the layers to move the overall class in a different direction.

There are many variations to the layers that might be added in this performance process. Here are some tools that may be added along the way:

- Movement
- Dialogue
- Narration
- Props/Costumes
- Musical accompaniment on instruments
- Prerecorded musical accompaniment
- Student-generated writing before, after, and/or during the performance
- Images projected in the background

- Sound effects
- Puppets
- Prerecorded students' stories or poems
- Large pieces of fabric
- One object (for instance, adding only a hat or a chair)

8

Reflection

"Take a Moment"

To make a prairie it takes a clover and one bee—
One clover, and a bee,
And revery.
The revery alone will do
If bees are few.

—EMILY DICKINSON

"We need to cultivate the art of self-overhearing," Tetlock says, "to learn how to eavesdrop on the mental conversations we have with ourselves."

—JONAH LEHRER

ONLY MINUTES REMAIN in this school day. Ordinarily, by 2:10 p.m. Jessica Costa's class of seventh grade English language learners at Calcutt Middle School would have been staring at the clock, waiting to be freed, stuffing work into backpacks, and pulling on coats despite Jessica's admonishment—"Wait. Class isn't over yet!"[1] But not today. Their backpacks remain untouched and their coats off as teaching artist John Holdridge begins a rhythmic clapping, the signal for them to "clap themselves into a circle." On seven previous visits to the class, John ended the day with this routine, and each time the students resisted, straggling slowly, half-heartedly into the circle, some remaining in corners leaning against desks. Today, however, no one hesitates. Today, they move quickly into a circle and match John's clapping until he gives the signal to stop. Following his instructions, everyone turns, their backs to the center and to one another.

"Take a moment to think of a few words you want to say to everyone about what you thought of today's class," John directs. "When you're ready, when you've got your words, turn and face the group."

After a moment's silence, the students face one another. One by one, they offer their thoughts: "There was energy." "We were focused." "Nobody fooled around." "We talked louder." "Everyone's getting better and better." "We were awesome."

Jessica steps forward. "What you did today was powerful. Moving. I understood what you were trying to say about *The Diary of Anne Frank*."

John is the last to speak. "Today we've achieved a new level. Today clicked. I'm so proud of you. This is our new starting point. I'd like you each to take a minute to think about what you did today that made today's class so good. Then I'd like you to think about what you can do tomorrow to make it even better." He pauses. "Remember, there is no going back. Everything starts from here and goes forward. "

The students absorb these words in silence. The bell rings, and in a swirl of activity they grab their backpacks and coats and hurry out the door.

One student remains behind and approaches John and Jessica. "I just want to say that I really like how we ended this class," he says.

Earlier in the day, as students were preparing tableaus to illustrate their responses to a section of *The Diary of Anne Frank,* John reminded them, "We *need* to hear your voices. You have things to tell us. Use your cafeteria voice. Your sports team voice. Your fight-with-your-brothers-and-sisters voice. Whatever voice you want to call it. Just let us hear you." The students responded to John's request as they presented their tableaus to one another, moving decisively and speaking loudly and clearly.

At the end of the class, in their standing circle, they marked their collective improvement. In the closing minutes of class, John gave them the time and space to recollect and share the successful practices that brought them to this level. Tomorrow, as John told them, that is where they would begin.

Days later, halfway across the country in Minnesota, in St. Paul's Central High School, Jan Mandell's intermediate acting students are also in a standing circle. As the class ends, Jan asks them to "circle up," requesting that each student step forward to point out a positive contribution someone else has made to the day's class.

Maisha steps forward. "Well, Dwayne had a really good idea when we were trying to figure out how to get all of us on stage at once." Dwayne nods and smiles. "And it worked."

Next, Jordon speaks up. "LaShawn helped me rehearse my lines and even suggested a way I could remember that hard part I'm always having trouble with."

One by one, students thank one another for small gestures, for making helpful suggestions, for offering solutions to performance problems, for supporting one another in obvious or subtle ways. Every day Jan's class ends with students sharing. Their comments are not always summaries of positive contributions. Sometimes they reflect on possible classroom improvements. Sometimes Jan asks them to identify the work to be done in tomorrow's class. Sometimes a student chooses the topic. They speak. They listen to one another. They make their voices heard. Jan and her students talk often about "creating safe space." By that they mean establishing an environment where everyone can trust, share, learn, and grow.

Sixth graders in another Minnesota classroom—this one in Minneapolis—sit in a half-circle, each student holding a copy of Emily Dickinson's poem beginning with the line "Hope is the thing with feathers" as they watch a group of peers under the direction of teaching artist Dudley Voigt perform an improvised version of the poem. Moments later, many raise their hands to respond to the prompt—"What did you notice?"—that their teacher, Veanne Beulter, gave them in advance of the performance. Students are familiar with the Critical Response Process originally developed by dancer and dance educator Liz Lerman and now being used by Mary Jo Thompson and others under the auspices of Minnesota's Perpich Center for Arts Education.[2] These educators adapted the protocol to center on four questions: What did you notice? What did you hear? What words or phrases resonated for you? Does this remind you of anything in your life? Designed to lead students to an in-depth investigation of an artwork, text, lesson, or performance, these questions have become a regular part of this group's classroom activities.

In Central Falls, Rhode Island, a class of elementary school students led by Elizabeth Keiser—all wearing matching orange t-shirts—finish a performance of their original work *The Ignor-Ant*. They remove their insect masks, sit down on the edge of the stage, and ask the audience, "What questions do you have for us?" They are prepared to explain their work and receive audience feedback.

In all these classes, students take the time to *reflect* on the collective work of the group and the contributions of specific individuals. Reflection that becomes a central feature of the learning environment sheds light on moments of individual learning and on ongoing relationships, events, or experiences; it helps students to develop what we teachers call *critical or higher-order thinking skills*.

REFLECTION AT THE CENTER

Derived from Latin, the word *reflection* relates to the act of "bending or turning (something) back, to give a backward bend or curve" and, more specifically, "to shine (light, a beam, a ray), esp. *on* or *upon* a person or thing."[3] As the term applies to the activity of the human mind, reflection describes thinking back on a particular subject carefully and deeply in order to illuminate or understand more fully. Reflection strategies play a central role in the Performance Cycle. As we use the term, reflecting refers to the act of turning back to think about content learned, one's mental processes, or the collective development of a community of learners.

We human beings have the ability to think about our thinking and actions, a quality that appears to distinguish us from other living beings. Philosopher and cognitive neuroscientist Andy Clark has argued that because human beings reflect, the learning process occurs not only inside the mind but in an "action loop" between the mind, body, and the outside world.[4] We act and simultaneously assess the outcomes of our actions. When we take note of the results, the knowledge gained feeds back into our cognition and affects our future actions. As Clark writes, "It is because we can think about our own thinking that we can actively structure our world in ways designed to promote, support, and extend our own cognitive achievements."[5] In putting our reflections in words, we create "the stable structure to which subsequent thinkings attach."[6] Neuroscience supports this claim. Laboratory research shows that learning can, in fact, change the brain's physical and organizational structures.[7]

Recently, teachers have applied cognitive theory to classrooms by emphasizing the role of *metacognition*—or thinking about thinking—in the learning process. Based on observations and conversations with teachers and students, we view *reflection* as encompassing an even wider territory, one that involves thinking beyond the self to contemplate the many links among the material being addressed, the self, and the group. As we define it, reflection explores what it means to learn in a specific social setting. If we view comprehension as incorporating content and metacognition as attending to one's own mental processes, then it seems logical to think of reflection as the ability to take in and consider the entire learning environment. As anyone who has observed classes in action knows, learning includes social as well as cognitive processes. By engaging in and mastering all three related aspects—comprehension, metacognition, and reflection—students develop not only knowledge but self-awareness, not only agency but judgment and wisdom. For this reason, we place reflection at the center of the Performance Cycle and at the heart of the project's approach to professional development for staff, teachers, and artists.

Understanding content—or, as we describe it in chapter 4, taking it, using it, and making it your own—is a central goal of work in classrooms. But the act of comprehension in its broadest sense need not and should not be seen as separate from reflection. Along with acquiring new knowledge, students benefit from recognizing the process by which they gain that knowledge. Similarly, for them to assume the agency to direct their learning as they mature, students must be able to identify the conditions, both internal and external, that best help them learn. Reflection aids comprehension across diverse disciplines and improves students' abilities to extend their learning to new settings.[8]

Reflection in its many forms may come before, during, and after an activity, a school day, or a final performance and may involve presenting and sharing ideas through writing, speaking, dance, improvisation, or visual art. When frequent and varied opportunities to reflect combine with ongoing curricular work, students have an opportunity to become more *mindful* of their own learning within the total learning environment.[9] The classroom climate becomes generative. Students improvise, create, revise, practice, and perform to the best of their abilities and continue to improve. In the process, they share a common experience. They focus their attention. They "look back" at their own work and the work of others and offer feedback and hear feedback from peers and teachers, artists and audience members. This combination of eyesight and insight produces powerful and memorable episodes of learning and has the potential to alter the motivation, engagement, and development not only of individuals but of the entire class.

THE *OTHELLO* STORY

Looking out from the stage into the dark, cavernous auditorium of the Nathanael Greene Middle School in Providence, Rhode Island, Theresa

Toomey Fox's students have much on their minds. Seated in the audience, family members, friends, and fellow students wait to see and hear the seventh graders offer their interpretation and response to Shakespeare's *Othello*. Six weeks ago, few of these students had heard of *Othello*, and most possessed only a passing familiarity with Shakespeare. While most *had* heard the name, they knew only that Shakespeare was somehow famous, lived "back in the day," and wrote in language that was hard to understand. They knew they would be expected to learn about him, but not just yet. Maybe later. Maybe in high school.

But here they stand—all eighty of them—on stage ready to perform *Give Me Moor Proof: Based on the Tragedy of* Othello *by William Shakespeare*. After a brief introduction, the entire sixth-period class steps forward to shout out their original song "I Shoulda Left You!" a modern-day imagining of Desdemona's dying thoughts. Next, one student offers a spirited rendition of Iago's monologue "I am not what I am" in precise Elizabethan English. Another class offers a choral reading of an original poem written by the students that begins "I am Iago."

Presented in twenty scenes, the *Othello* performance features everyone in Theresa's four classes speaking, dancing, and performing. Students offer classic monologues by Desdemona, Emilia, and Othello direct from the text. Individually and chorally in their own language, they describe and interpret the characters, outline the plot, and offer a modern-day retelling and commentary.

While the act of studying *Othello* may seem unusual and challenging for seventh graders, few other texts so vividly present themes and topics young adolescents deal with every day: jealousy, rumors, gossip, trust, revenge, racism. Students face these issues regularly, though on a far less heroic scale. The scope of the challenge and the themes in the text provide a perfect vehicle for the work Theresa's students do. By introducing *Othello*, she expects students to examine the plot, theme, language, and background of this classic tragedy; establish connections between the texts and issues in their own lives and the world; and present these ideas in several different kinds of performances of understanding. Simultaneously, she expects them to develop the cognitive skills to grapple with challenging text as well as an increased awareness of the workings of their minds and a sense of what methods best make them effective learners. Finally, she expects them to develop an awareness of the complex aspects of the work of the entire class, to collaborate with one another, and to contribute positively to the learning of the classroom community. To accomplish all this, she places reflection at the center of the unit from the very first day.

As each student enters the classroom in January, Theresa hands out a sheet of paper that looks like a quiz (see figure 8.1). The first true or false question on the "quiz" titled "Breakin' Up Is Hard to Do" reads, "It is better to dump someone than to have them dump you." Other statements read, "It's okay to hurt someone in self-defense," and "You should 'stick to your own kind' when looking for someone to love." Students are surprised

FIGURE 8.1
The *Othello* quiz: Breakin' up is hard to do

True or false:
1. ___ It is better to dump someone than to have him or her dump you.
2. ___ If someone lies to you once, there is no way you can trust him or her again.
3. ___ To get to the top, sometimes you have to step on people.
4. ___ It is OK to hurt people if they break the law.
5. ___ Hate will make you crazy.
6. ___ If you are angry with someone, you should hit him or her.
7. ___ It is OK to hurt people in self-defense.
8. ___ You should "stick to your own kind" when looking for someone to love.
9. ___ If you love somebody you would never cheat on him or her.
10. ___ You should have something in common with the person you love.
11. ___ Wives should obey their husbands.
12. ___ It is OK to hurt people if they hurt your feelings.
13. ___ You can love someone and hate him or her at the same time.
14. ___ Love will make you crazy.
15. ___ You cannot love someone you cannot trust.
16. ___ You can love someone from a different race or culture.
17. ___ If someone takes something you own, you can use violence to get it back.
18. ___ Sometimes things are too good to be true.
19. ___ You can be innocent of a crime because of temporary insanity.

and intrigued. The quiz is unlike any they had ever taken. No teacher had ever asked them to offer their written opinions on friendship, trust, gossip, or love.

Theresa instructs the class to answer the questions independently, as they would any other classroom quiz. When they finish, she divides the students into small groups to discuss their answers and explain their thinking. It doesn't take long before lively—at times heated—debate springs up around the classroom. The surveys, or "opinionaires," become the first item in each student's individual *Othello* portfolio, and the topics addressed come up often as the class reads the play. After reading, they return to the quiz and compile the class's responses, discussing and debating the many possible interpretations of each statement. Beginning the unit with the opinionaire encourages students to consider their own thinking and beliefs in relation to the text's important themes and other people's responses. Writing down and sharing these beliefs in groups clarifies them in a way that encourages periodic reexamination. As they read the text, they revisit the questions to note how the themes develop in relation to their own recorded beliefs. Opening the conversation up to the entire class allows students to see the learning process as it occurs not only on an individual level but also as a community-wide event.

As with the classroom activities, many of the homework assignments help students comprehend the text and organize and monitor their own thinking. One handout, for example, includes a simple three-column form. The play's seven major characters are listed in the first column. For homework, the students fill in the second column—"What character wants"—and a third column—"Supporting lines from the text." The assignment provides a structure for making interpretations and identifying what has led them to their understandings. Other graphic organizers provide a similar strategy for noting key passages, paraphrasing Shakespeare's Elizabethan language, creating plot timelines, charting character development, and generating a cogent and coherent argument for an analytic essay. These assignments serve both to further students' comprehension of the text and to help them recognize and explain their own thought processes. In this way they learn about *Othello* and, simultaneously, their own learning processes.

Many assignments feature rubrics showing students the criteria for excellent work, thus providing feedback on their participation in the learning process. One rubric offers criteria for effective rehearsal and performance. Developed by the students themselves, this rubric focuses students on the "four Cs": cooperation, commitment, creativity, and clarity (see "For the Classroom"). Creating and completing these rubrics encourages students to *look back* and document their own progress and contributions to the work of the group. Students reflect on their accomplishments to determine in real and personal ways what their efforts might mean both to them and others in the class. Halfway through the *Othello* unit, students take a practice test for the statewide writing assessment. Rather than shift away from the topic, Theresa developed a series of essay prompts linking *Othello*'s plot and themes to issues in students' lives. One prompt asks students to consider the importance of trust in relationships, asking them, "What is trust? What is important about trust in relationships? How do people develop trust?" A second prompt asks them to consider things they've done and later regretted, offering as examples Cassio being persuaded to drink and Emilia being convinced to steal Desdemona's handkerchief. A third prompt asks students to consider Iago's famous phrases "Men should be what they seem" (III.iii) and "I am not what I am" (I.i) in relation to themselves and their experiences with other people. In these essays, students write vividly about misunderstandings, intrigues, loss of trust, and a range of life's complexities. They produce personal versions of the grand themes of the play. In this way, they reflect on the text in relation to their own experiences, transferring the classroom learning to their own lives.

At the conclusion of the unit, the students revisit their completed portfolios and respond to the question, "What did you get out of doing *Othello* the way we did?" This assignment gives students the chance to review the unit, reexamine their work, and consider how their understanding has developed. The overwhelming majority comment on specific activities, their attitudes toward the work of the class, personal changes they noticed throughout the unit, and the effect they imagine their learning might have on their futures. Several students identified an improved attitude toward schoolwork that would—or already had—carried over to other classes. One student wrote,

> I now find it much easier to read primary source documents when I have to do a project for social studies or some other class. The final performance was awesome. To take a play that is hundreds of years old and modernize it into language that I can understand seems hard at first. But seeing everybody get on stage and actually do it made me know it's not impossible. Even if the script is old, it can totally relate to today's society.

Many expressed surprise at having developed strong personal interests and connections that motivated their learning.

> If I had never read this play, when I went to the library I would never think about getting a book like this. Now, I would and that's good because it helps me when I have to read something I don't want to in school.
>
> At first I thought, well, I'm just going to take advantage of a fun class. But by the end of it, I realized even though I had a lot of fun, it was the most learning I'd done this year.

Others identified life lessons they took from the play.

> It made me think, "Well, if that ever happened to me, what would I do?" It also made me think of more obvious things to do instead of making it a tragedy.
>
> I learned you should never believe what you hear and only half of what you see. Because if you don't you can always end up just like Othello and his ... very sad story.

A number of students commented on what they gained from performing.

> I saw how my classmates were really good at acting certain characters in the play. My own acting helped me to understand more.
>
> Instead of reading the play (which we did but we had fun), we *were* the play. We performed monologues, discussed each scene, acted and other

activities. It was fun how we did it. I also improved my acting skills when we performed the final montage . . . Oh, and I understood the story.

Many wrote of changed relationship with peers.

I got to experience the book with the other students and see what their thoughts and ideas were.

By working in groups, I was able to see what other students thought about the play and how they anticipated (what would happen in) the book.

Before I used to be a shy quiet person that nobody knew. But as time progressed, I was comfortable with the people I worked with. As I got used to that, I talked louder and more and I'm not really that shy anymore.

A few identified the project's potential lasting effect on their future.

I want to be a teacher when I get older and I learned that this way to teach seems to help kids to understand.

It showed me how to trust your heart and believe in the one you love. It also shows me that reading and acting could be a big part of my life if I involve myself in it more.

Not all of the student feedback proved positive. A few did not identify any personal connection to course content. One student responded honestly, "The only thing I got out of reading the play was the fact that I am proud of myself for reading a Shakespeare play." However, even this response showed honesty and considerable self-awareness. This student had come to take personal pride in reading a challenging text. Developing a sense of pride in completing difficult work—particularly when that work does not spark a personal passion—represents a noble and important gain. Identifying and reflecting on this gain may help this student transfer and extend what he learned to other academic, personal, or professional pursuits.

For Theresa, these final reflections had benefits for her as a learner and teacher. Reading these responses, she learned what worked well and what did not and why. She used this knowledge to improve her teaching practice and, specifically, to revise her curriculum. Reflection of this sort benefits learners at every stage of development. For this reason, reflection is not only the center of work with students but with teachers and artists as well.

REFLECTION: COMING FULL CIRCLE

Content knowledge, certainly, but also differences in reflective practice separate novices from experts. Experts have learned how best to listen to their past gains and mistakes in order to change their future actions. In *How We Decide*, Jonah Lehrer writes that "even the most attentive and self-aware minds will still make mistakes . . . But the best decision-makers do not despair. Instead, they become students of error, determined to learn from what went wrong. They think about what they could have done differently so that the next time their neurons will know what to do."[10] A body of research supports the finding that successful learners engage in an ongoing study of their errors and achievements. People of all ages benefit from this type of reflection, looking back at what led them to their own learning. "This is the most astonishing thing about the human brain: it can always improve itself. Tomorrow, we can make better decisions."[11]

In schools, reflective practice has the potential to extend beyond the personal to the larger social realm. Adolescents are particularly suited to learning by sharing reflections with groups of their peers. Young teens are still developing the skills to reason, plan, monitor, and assess their thinking. Most are eager to see inside the minds of others in order to understand their thoughts and emotions. For this reason, they read one another keenly, seeking clues to construct their lives from clothes, music, activities, and attitudes. Conversation can serve as guideposts to their classmates' minds as well. In theory, classrooms function as environments for students to discuss and share their diverse perspectives and thought processes, to have moments of self-discovery as well as insights into how other people think and learn.

In practice, educators often fail to provide students with helpful opportunities to reflect on learning as a group. The most common content-related conversations in classrooms take the form of exchanges between the teacher and individual students. In these exchanges, known in education circles as IRE (Initiation, Response, Evaluation), a teacher asks a question, receives a brief response from a student, approves or disapproves of the response's correctness, and, if incorrect, addresses the question to another student, the purpose being to push the student toward the "right" answer.[12] In an attempt to surpass the limits of IRE, educators have developed a wide variety of strategies and protocols to help students write and speak more fully and meaningfully when exploring topics (see chapter 4). Each of these strategies does have the potential to deepen the role of reflection in schools, but no formula by itself can create a rich, comprehensive learning environment.

Most adolescents are eager to know what their peers think, but oftentimes nothing intimidates students more than figuring out what to think and what to say when asked to present their thoughts in classroom conversation. To establish a classroom climate that fosters reflection in the broadest sense, students must discover they can share their thoughts, insights, and questions without fear of judgment. When the social norms of the classroom invite and support ongoing reflection, students will focus, participate, observe, and comment, assuming the role of teacher as well as learner. Class members have opportunities to listen to and come to know one another by sharing observations, feelings, and interpretations. They identify issues the class needs to address. They comment appropriately and responsibly, giving useful and pertinent feedback to themselves and others. In the hands of a skilled facilitator, reflection promotes solidarity and strengthens the classroom community.

If the learning environment invites multiple perspectives, encouraging students to become active listeners and confident presenters, the teacher-student dichotomy diminishes as the entire class teaches and learns from one another. Through building and growing as a community and moving through each element of the Performance Cycle, students enter and develop in a space that feels both safe and encouraging. With reflection at the center of their efforts, they become their own best teachers.

The forms that ongoing reflection take in classrooms closely connect to the concept of mindfulness, in which environments support participants in "developing the creation of new categories; openness to new information; and an implicit awareness of more than one perspective."[13] Research on mindfulness suggests that the

> educational potential of mindfulness lies in . . . addressing some of the other intractable problems of education such as the flexible transfer of skills and knowledge to new contexts, the development of deep understanding, student motivation and engagement, the ability to think critically and creatively, and the development of more self-directed learners.[14]

Further, this work suggests that classroom practices such as those developed by Theresa Fox and the other teachers whose stories we tell in this book have the capacity to help learners develop the disposition toward mindfulness, "a consistently enabling state . . . in which individuals tend to feel more in control of their lives."[15]

REFLECTION: AN ENDING AND A BEGINNING

Reflection instills hope at the center of our work because it encourages a sense of optimism, a roadmap for the future, and an ongoing opportunity to learn. Reflection helps us take note of our current situation, how we arrived here, and who we might be tomorrow. At the outset of this book, we told the story of Anthony, the young man who on the first day of school imagines the year ahead as a constant struggle to stay awake in class. We asked the educators among us to imagine the world from Anthony's perspective and to address the question, "How can we create a learning environment that students—including Anthony—find relevant, challenging, and worthy of their attention and effort?" The work of the New London Group, educator Paulo Freire, philosopher Maxine Greene, and linguist Shirley Brice Heath encourages us to help Anthony develop the "ability to imagine it could be otherwise" in order to "construct a positive social future" for himself and others like him.[16] We can think of no topic more worthy of our reflection and, subsequently, our action. As John Holdridge suggests to his class at the outset of this chapter, we believe that helping Anthony learn to reflect on that question offers us a new place to begin—"everything starts from here and goes forward."

FOR THE CLASSROOM

REFLECTION

Back to Front

Developed by Jan Mandell, Back to Front is a useful activity for reflecting on a lengthy process. Often it's been used immediately after students have completed a performance or participated in a public exhibit of their work. The purpose is for participants to offer a spontaneous reflection on the previous experience.

Five students stand in the front of the class in a horizontal line with their backs to the audience. In a random order, each student turns and faces the audience and speaks. Only one person faces the audience at a given moment. When one person turns toward the audience, the other quickly turns away from the audience. Students will need to listen carefully to each other and work as an ensemble to ensure that only one person is facing the audience at any given moment. They must do this with no touching, no cues, and no looking or talking to each other.

As the first person turns to the front, she offers her reflection and continues to talk until another person chooses to turn forward. The first speaker then turns away and the new speaker takes over with his or her own train of thought.

You might want to instruct, "Speakers may not cross reference each other, but must focus on your own train of thought." Or you might ask speakers to connect their comments to previous remarks. After a few minutes, another group of five stands in front of the class and repeats the process.

Chalk Talk

Chalk talk is a way of brainstorming without talking. Write on the center of the board a key word, idea, or question and place a circle around it.

The word or phrase should be a large concept that demands exploring and uncovering. In a recent unit on teaching *Hamlet* to a group of high school students, teaching artist Steve Kidd ended a class by reading students the famous line, "O God, I could be bounded in a nutshell, and count myself a king of infinite space—were it not that I have bad dreams." He then asked them to turn their attention to a sheet of chart paper on the back wall of the auditorium stage where they had been practicing key scenes from the play. At the center of the paper Steve had written the word *trapped*. One by one, students stepped forward, took up a marker, and created a concept map that summarized their thoughts on the word. They would use these words in the next day's class to begin a piece of writing in which they reflected on Hamlet's situation.

This activity is conducted in silence. Students step up, write their comments, and then return to their seats. They may add thoughts or questions about the word or phrase someone has written previously by drawing a line and adding their own comment. The rest of the class observes the silent conversation taking place on the board and contributes whenever a piece of chalk becomes available. At the end of the activity, a concept map should fill the board.

If a rich conversation emerges on the board, use written phrases or dialogue to spark a verbal exploration of the topic. However, often when students do this activity the first time in a class, they may not fully invest in it, and the concepts outlined on the board may be somewhat superficial. If this is the case, use it as an opportunity. Ask the questions: When was the conversation most effective? When was it not? If we were to do this activity again what would it take to succeed?

From Beginning to End

In Theresa Toomey Fox's middle school classroom, her students keep all their work in folders in the classroom. At the end of the year, she has her students take out their folders. They look at the scope of their work throughout the year and reflect on how they've grown and what they've learned. She has them put their reflections in writing and share them with the class.

Circle Reflection

To reflect on a day's class and to bring a sense of closure to an experience, ask the students to gather in a standing circle. (Teaching artist John Holdridge has them "clap into a circle" by clapping their hands continuously until the circle forms.) Ask the students to turn their backs to one another and think about one of the following prompts (for the prompts requiring text, they will need to have the text in hand):

- What is one word you would use to describe today's experience?
- What is something you appreciate today from one of your classmates?
- What is a positive contribution one of your classmates made to today's class?
- Find a phrase you like from the text we read today and share it with the group.
- Find a phrase from your own writing and share it with the group.

The students turn around and share their selected phrases with one another.

Ensemble Essentials

No matter how old or young you are, you are likely to find it's not easy to work with a group of people. For years we have placed youth and adults in groups together and the same challenges emerge: one person feels they need to direct the rest of the group, one person never talks and is never asked her opinion, two people have widely divergent views about the process and become entrenched in their positions, or one person in the group gets offended and shuts down.

In order to avoid these potential pitfalls, before asking people to work in groups creating a performance or another piece of work, we ask them to develop *ensemble essentials*, a set of criteria, or a rubric, for reflecting on the ongoing work of the group.

Ask the entire group, "What are the essential elements required for working effectively together?" Allow the group to call out ideas and capture them on the board. In a recent workshop with graduate students in education at Harvard University, the students came up with the following:

- Build on each other's comments by saying "Yes, and . . ."; don't negate what another person says
- Spend more time creating than talking
- Listen to each other; try not to focus on what you want to say next
- Value everyone in the group as an expert
- Create space for the quiet person

Theresa Toomey Fox's middle school students developed the following essentials that were more aimed at the individual's contribution to the overall group:

Cooperation
- You contributed positively to your group
- You worked hard to develop ideas and were always willing to try the ideas of others
- You used your time efficiently and were focused on the work at hand
- You avoided being distracted or distracting others in their work

Commitment
- You took yourself and your role seriously
- You gave energy, emotion and focus to your role

Creativity
- You used different emotional and physical levels in your performances
- You always tried new ideas to enhance your performance

Clarity
- You could be heard and understood
- Your performance effectively communicated to the audience the major ideas of the scene or text

Divide the class into small ensembles. Before working on the creative task at hand, ask each group to look at the Ensemble Essentials developed by the larger class and modify them so that all members of the group are in agreement before the work begins.

At the beginning or end of a workday, ask the group to return to the set of essentials. Did they succeed at the essentials? Are there areas they could improve on next time? Are there essentials they would like to change based on the dynamics of the group?

Capangas

Capangas is a process for reflecting on the work of a group at the end of an experience. We first used capangas for all of our teachers and teaching artists at the end of our first Brown Summer High School in Brazil. Capangas was developed by Daniel Soares, whose students created the cordel around the lake in his town of Inhumas.

Capanga is a Portuguese word referring to a small bag usually used by fisherman for fishing. Daniel explains,

> When I thought of this activity, I thought about the fisherman and how he keeps the very important things in this bag that he needs for fishing, for sustaining himself, when he is at a river, far from the city. If we take life of a teacher as the metaphor, then you would need a capanga always. And what do we keep in these capangas? We keep all the precious moments we live together as a community, so, when any thing in life happens to make us want to give up, we can go back to our capangas to find what makes us strong and makes us want to keep going in life as a teacher.

At the end of the summer, Daniel had a capanga made for every person. These weren't expensive, luxury bags but simple bags made from potato sacks. Each was labeled with a teacher's name.

Next to the bags were pencils and a stack of postcard-size papers. Daniel asked all of us to write a letter to each person in the group about our experience with that person over the summer and then to put these letters inside that person's capanga. After about an hour, we each picked up our capanga filled with letters and read what others had written about us. We gathered in a circle and each shared a postcard written about us to end the summer program.

This activity works best after a meaningful time that students have spent together—creating a performance, participating in summer program, or working together throughout the year in the classroom.

Idea Mapping

A Google search of *mind mapping* or *idea mapping* will reveal a wealth of possibilities and models to share with students (one, the Chalk Talk, is previously described). The core idea is to make thinking around a particular subject or concept visible in the form of an aesthetically pleasing object. Students might create maps individually, in small groups, or as an entire class.

In one technique, begin with a sheet of paper positioned horizontally, in the landscape position. Begin with an image in the center of the paper that captures the core idea. Then have students create branches of ideas off of the center concept and sub-branches, either describing them with words or images. Continue until the paper is full.

At a teacher institute led by an arts-integration organization called SmART Schools, Rhode Island School of Design professor Amy Leidtke used a mind map to respond to an essay we read by naturalist Barry Lopez called "Landscape and Narrative" in his book *Crossing Open Ground*. Amy had arranged large foam core sheets on the tables of her classroom, and participants used markers to map their understanding of the text primarily through images (they used only a few words). Midway through the process, Amy asked them to stand back and look at their idea maps, prompting them to reflect on what they had created so far and asking how they might bring the disparate parts of their maps together. She encouraged them to fill the entire space and leave minimal white space. The result was an interesting collective artistic piece as well as a shared representation of the students' understanding of the text.

The difference between this activity and Chalk Talk is that the participants talk and plan as part of the process. The idea is to create an aesthetic object that compellingly communicates the ideas of the group.

Speaking Through the Image

Speaking Through the Image is a tool that can be used at the beginning or the end of a process. Collect a variety of images. (This reflection activity actually works better if the images don't have any direct relation to the topic.) Place the images in the center of the room. Ask the students to choose the image that best represents the topic or experience for them and share with each other in pairs, small groups, or an entire class their image and their response to the image in terms of the topic.

We've used Speaking Through the Image in many classes as a way to enter a topic. For instance, one of Kurt's language classes in Mexico was reading the book *To Kill a Mockingbird*. The class that week was exploring the concept of *otherness* and how it feels to be left out of a group. Kurt placed a variety of photographs by Robert Frank in the center of the table and asked the students in the class to each choose a photograph they thought best represented feeling left out.

Speaking Through the Image might also be used to reflect on an experience. When we are at art museums, we often buy postcards of visual art to use for this activity. We scatter the postcards on the floor in the classroom and at the end of the semester ask students to choose a work of visual art that best represents their experience during the semester. Students share their images and their thoughts about the semester.

Epilogue

One Step at a Time

FOR THE PAST TEN YEARS, we have gathered activities that link the arts and literacy, some that we created, some that we learned from artist and teacher colleagues. We have designed curriculum and shared our materials widely in workshops and on our project Web site. This book moves beyond sharing activities to discuss the *why* as well as the *how*. Through stories of exemplary ArtsLiteracy work in classrooms around the world, we show how the arts and literacy can be combined in ways that are deeply meaningful to students and teachers alike. We particularly want to position this work in the larger fields of literacy pedagogies, arts education, and education practice and policy, describing the theory behind the practice and showing models of the work.

In so doing, we also want to challenge the seemingly relentless press toward uniformity that appears to be winning the day in education circles. As an alternative, we want to propose that educators seek a balance between uniformity and diversity, between establishing fixed learning standards and honoring the innovation, exploration, and unique context that marks every classroom environment. We question the value for either students or teachers of the "same day, same page" approach to curriculum. Rather than mandating and implementing a tightly linked top-down system of standardized curriculum and testing, we support an approach that gives greater weight to substantive, ongoing, well-supported teacher preparation and professional development and that promotes school-based decision making, curriculum, and assessment.

To participate honestly and with integrity in a conversation about how best to establish this balance, we must begin by acknowledging that teaching in classrooms where engaged and active learning is going on is extremely challenging work. To plan and implement instruction that inspires a class full of reluctant students to get out of their seats; take ownership of their work with maturity, focus, and effort; collaborate; take risks; work hard and consistently; go public with the results; and reflect on the entire endeavor may be far riskier and more demanding than approaches that ask far less of students.

We were reminded of this point just recently after a workshop we led for a group of teachers. Not surprisingly, in the workshop, the teachers enthusiastically embraced the work, behaved perfectly, did exactly what we asked them to do, attended carefully to our instructions, and created an impressive and memorable performance. They left the workshop fully inspired and ready to take these ideas to their classroom. Yet, one week later we received the following e-mail from a frustrated teacher:

> Have been teaching my 10th grade students some performances exercises. I really love these ideas and they really give me something to work on. However, the class is loaded with behavioral challenges. There is a lot of oppositional defiance, side-talking and they are loud. Are there any strategies that you found successful with an unruly classroom using integrated performance art? This has been a real struggle.

The message of our workshops—and of this book—is unambiguous: *establish an environment in which students are active, engaged, and performing meaningful work.* In these pages, we share some of the best ideas we've seen. Yet we know that the practices we describe require time and preparation to implement successfully. Learning to teach well is the work of a lifetime. A teacher's skills develop as the result of millions of interactions within a community of learners, both peers and students.

In an e-mail, Dan DeCelles, a veteran teacher whose middle school serves students from immigrant, high-poverty backgrounds, wrote about his ongoing effort to shape and sharpen his own teaching practice:

> ArtsLiteracy challenges us to change what school is and what school means, not just how school is done. And change is hard. But we're talking about battles that need to be fought, to keep kids from falling through the cracks and to keep schools, especially high-poverty urban schools, from continuing to fail students. Approaches of this sort involve a fundamental, if not revolutionary, change in the roles and relationships between teacher and students in the classroom.
>
> Great teachers understand this challenge is part of their own continued learning, in the same vein that we ask our students to take risks and possibly fail—then, the next day, pick ourselves up and try again. And try again. And again.[1]

How, in the current climate and present circumstances, is a teacher to attempt such continued efforts? Experience tells us that it helps to be in a supportive environment in which teachers and students are respected and encouraged to take initiative and to innovate. It helps to have time to plan and to respond to student work. It helps to have role models to inspire and to turn to for advice and coaching. It helps to have interested colleagues who listen, help, even co-teach. It helps to have partners and collaborators such as teaching artists. It helps to have ongoing professional development that holds everyone to mutually agreed-on standards and offers models and samples of excellent teaching.

Experience also tells us that, although certainly more difficult, some teachers achieve considerable success working entirely on their own. When adapting the ideas of this book to the classroom, we encourage you to start where you are most comfortable and begin with approaches you know will work for your particular groups of students. If you are a teacher who is terrified of getting the students up out of their seats, then begin with comprehension and creation and work gradually toward performance.

Offer a space for your students to read, write, and talk. Then, as the work progresses, create small performance groups. The students can plan in their seats and put the performance on its feet when they—and you—are comfortable doing so.

The ArtsLiteracy Project has become a community of teachers, artists, and students working with a set of ideas and figuring out the best way to move forward. The ideas in this book are meant to be adapted to many contexts. The pedagogy of the project is ever evolving; it lives in the artists, teachers, and students who helped shape it over the years and continues to evolve in schools and other settings around the globe. Shirley Brice Heath uses the term *platform* to describe such an organization, in that it is a delineated space for people with a shared interest.[2] Steven Johnson refers to this type of space as a *liquid network,* a collection of individuals that formally and informally exchange and build on each other's ideas.[3]

The Performance Cycle grew, over time, out of the environments we designed for collaboration among teachers, artists, and students. In the spirit of the pedagogies in this book, artists and teachers formed partnerships with a clear goal of finding new and effective ways to teach literacy in our schools. We were on a journey together, creating the road as we went along, giving everyone in the community, regardless of age or experience, the opportunity to offer ideas and even to change the direction of the enterprise. This shared effort is what gives the ArtsLiteracy Project its life and vibrancy. Those who contributed are numerous, and many are highlighted in these pages.

We hope this book helps us all take another step, and we invite you into the conversation online at www.artslit.org, a forum for continuing, in poet Antonio Machado's words, to make the road by walking.

> Wanderer, your footsteps are
> the road, and nothing more;
> wanderer, there is no road,
> the road is made by walking.

By walking one makes the road,
and upon glancing behind
one sees the path
that never will be trod again.
Wanderer, there is no road
Only wakes upon the sea.[4]

Notes

Introduction

1. Anthony is a composite of many students we have known and taught. In the chapters that follow, the real names of students, teachers, and artists are used except in a few cases where we use a pseudonym for reasons of confidentiality. These will be clearly indicated.

2. Wiske, *Teaching for Understanding.*

3. UN Population Commission, *Report,* 17–18.

4. Gee, "What Is Literacy?"

5. New London Group, "A Pedagogy of Multiliteracies," 64.

6. Gee, "What Is Literacy?" 3.

7. Greene, *Releasing the Imagination,* 1.

8. New London Group, "A Pedagogy of Multiliteracies," 67.

9. Ravitch, *Death and Life,* 229.

10. Freire, *Pedagogy of the Oppressed,* 72.

11. Horton, Freire, Bell, Gaventa, and Peters, *We Make the Road,* 77–78.

12. Greene, *Releasing the Imagination,* 15, 19, 4, 10.

13. Heath, "Imaginative Actuality," 27, 28.

14. See, for example, Snow, Porche, Tabors, and Harris, *Is Literacy Enough?*

15. The Performance Cycle was created by Eileen Landay and Kurt Wootton in 1999.

16. González, Moll, and Amanti, *Funds of Knowledge*; Moll and Greenberg, "Creating Zones of Possibility."

17. Wootton, "Community This and Community That."

18. Anderson and Krathwohl, *A Taxonomy for Learning*.

19. Cushman, *Fires in the Mind*, 97–98.

Chapter 1

1. Russell is a pseudonym.

2. Bobby Marchand, interview with Kurt Wootton, January 27, 2011.

3. Gardner, *Multiple Intelligences*.

4. Shirley Brice Heath addressed this topic in detail in *Ways with Words*, a landmark study of the language socialization of children from different sociocultural groups and the impact of that socialization on children's school experiences.

5. Sarah Blakely-Cummings, "Feliciliteracy," unpublished paper, Brown University, 2005.

6. Students in the ArtsLiteracy Project's Brazil Lab School, piloted in July 2006, used the word *alegria* to describe their learning experiences, defining it as containing elements of joy, happiness, and celebration.

7. Lave and Wenger, *Situated Learning*.

8. Wenger, *Communities of Practice*, 1.

9. Lee and Smagorinsky, *Vygotskian Perspectives*, 5.

10. Mandell and Wolf, *Acting, Learning and Change*, 2.

11. Seligman, *Helplessness*.

12. Sizer, *The Red Pencil*; Wiggins and McTighe, *Understanding by Design*.

13. Wiggins, "What Is an Essential Question?"

14. Wilhelm, *"You Gotta BE the Book."*

15. Anderson, *Research Foundations*.

16. Stanovich, *Matthew Effects*.

17. Rosenblatt, *Reader, Text, Poem*.

18. Marchand interview.

19. Greene, *Releasing the Imagination,* 15.

20. Martin, *Mostly About Writing.*

21. For more on this point, see, for example, Podlozny, "Strengthening Verbal Skills"; Wagner, *Educational Drama and Language Arts*; Wilhelm, *"You Gotta BE the Book";* Wolf, Edmiston, and Enciso, "Drama Worlds."

22. Heath, "Imaginative Actuality."

23. Sizer, *The Red Pencil;* Wiske, *Teaching for Understanding.*

24. Bransford, Brown, and Cocking, *How People Learn;* Schön, *The Reflective Practitioner.*

25. Clark, *Being There,* 208–210.

26. Egan, *Imagination in Teaching and Learning.*

27. Donald, *Origins of the Modern Mind.*

Chapter 2

1. Slater, *Stories on a String.*

2. Ibid., 30.

3. Daniel Soares, interview with Kurt Wootton, June 2008.

4. Soares interview.

5. Soares interview.

6. Soares interview.

7. Atwell, *Reading Zone,* 21.

8. See, for example, Bakhtin, *Dialogic Imagination;* Gee, *Social Linguistics and Literacies;* Landay, "Performance as the Foundation"; Lave and Wenger, *Situated Learning.*

9. Smith, *Joining the Literacy Club.*

10. Sizer, *Horace's School,* 26.

11. Mateus Rodriguez, e-mail to Daniel Soares, February 2006.

12. Nieto, *Light in Their Eyes,* 93–94.

13. Ibid., 93.

14. Garcia Lorca, *Blood Wedding.*

15. Boal, *Games for Actors and Non-Actors.*

16. Ferreiro, *Past and Present;* Rosenblatt, *Reader, Text, Poem.*

17. Wilhelm, *"You Gotta BE the Book,"* 85.

18. Horton, Freire, Bell, Gaventa, and Peters, *We Make the Road,* 38.

19. Soares interview.

20. See Atkins, *improv!;* Boal, *Games for Actors and Non-Actors;* Heathcote and Bolton, *Drama for Learning;* Mandell and Wolf, *Acting, Learning and Change;* Rohd, *Theater for Community;* Spolin, *Improvisation for the Theater;* Zaporah, *Action Theater: The Improvisation of Presence.*

21. Smyth and Stevenson, *You Want to Be Part of Everything,* 22.

Chapter 3

1. Boal, *Games for Actors and Non-Actors.*

2. Wilson, *Piano Lesson,* 42.

3. Rumi, *Essential Rumi,* 36.

4. Goodlad, *A Place Called School,* 242.

5. Ornstein and Levine, *Foundations of Education,* 300–301.

6. Greene, *Releasing the Imagination,* 26.

7. Donald, *Origins of the Modern Mind.*

8. Douglass, *Narrative;* Obama, *Dreams from my Father.*

9. Obama, "A More Perfect Union."

10. Goldin-Meadow, *Hearing Gesture.*

11. Ibid., x.

12. Bennett, "Don't Just Stand There."

13. King, *Storymaking and Drama,* 162.

14. Perkins, *Smart Schools.*

15. Wiggins, "What Is an Essential Question?"

16. Clifton, "whose side are you on?"

17. Robinson, *Unlocking Shakespeare's Language.*

18. Cisneros, *House on Mango Street*, 3.

19. Common Core State Standards Initiative, http://www.corestandards. org/the-standards/english-language-arts-standards/anchor-standards-6-12/ college-and-career-readiness-anchor-standards-for-reading/.

20. Cisneros, *House on Mango Street*, 3.

21. Ibid., 4–5.

22. Ibid., 5.

Chapter 4

1. All names in this vignette are pseudonyms.

2. Tan, *Joy Luck Club*, 134.

3. Mehan, *Learning Lessons*.

4. Anderson and Krathwohl, *Taxonomy for Learning*.

5. *Oxford English Dictionary* online edition.

6. See, for example, Harvey and Goudvis, *Strategies That Work*.

7. See, for example, Beers, Probst, and Reif, *Adolescent Literacy;* Keene and Zimmerman, *Mosaic of Thought;* Gallagher, *Deeper Reading*.

8. Khymyle Mims, e-mail to Maggie Blake, March 2008, emphasis added.

9. Cornelius Rish, interview with Eileen Landay, August 2008.

10. Heath, *Ways with Words*, 49, 70.

11. Kress, *Literacy in the New Media Age*.

12. Greenfield, *Technology and Informal Education*.

13. Ibid., 71.

14. National Endowment for the Arts, *To Read or Not*, 9.

15. Conley, *College Knowledge*.

16. Rish interview.

17. Mims e-mail.

18. Clara Hutchinson, interview with Eileen Landay, May 2008.

19. Reddy, "Conduit Metaphor."

20. Matthew Shipman, interview with Eileen Landay, August 2008.

21. Donald, "Art and Cognitive Evolution."

22. Clark, *Being There,* 53, 35–36.

23. Anthony Jacobs, interview with Eileen Landay, August 2008.

24. The I-Search paper was initially developed and described in Macrorie, *The I-Search Paper,* and has since become a staple high school and college writing assignment.

25. Hutchinson interview.

26. Mai Lee Khang, unpublished paper, St. Paul Public Schools, May 2008.

27. Firaol Adam, unpublished paper, St. Paul Public Schools, May 2008.

Chapter 5

1. Whitman, *Poetry and Prose,* 297.

2. Pink, *Whole New Mind,* 27.

3. Florida, *Rise of the Creative Class,* 44.

4. Davidson, *Now You See It,* 77–78.

5. Freire, *Pedagogy of Freedom,* 111.

6. Whitman, *Poetry and Prose,* 8–9.

7. Ibid., 672.

8. Ferreiro, *Past and Present,* 69.

9. Pew Hispanic Center, *Hispanics,* 2.

10. Nieto, *Light in Their Eyes,* 8.

11. Whitman, *Poetry and Prose,* 247.

12. Koch, *Wishes, Lies and Dreams,* 3.

13. Atwell, *In the Middle.*

14. Atwell, *Lessons That Change Writers.*

15. Ewald, *Secret Games.*

16. Said, *Humanism and Democratic Criticism,* 76.

17. Freire, *Education for Critical Consciousness.*

18. Whitman, *Poetry and Prose,* 188.

19. Wolf, Edmiston, and Enciso, "Drama Worlds."

20. Lee, *To Kill a Mockingbird,* 20.

21. Freire, *Pedagogy of Hope,* 90.

22. Rosenblatt, *Literature as Exploration,* 7.

23. Steinbeck, *The Pearl,* 8.

Chapter 6

1. Excerpt from an e-mail exchange between Karla Hernando and Jessica Robertson, October 25, 2010.

2. See chapter 2 for a description of Daniel Soares's ArtsLiteracy work in Brazil.

3. Comments made by Jessica Robertson and Karla Hernando throughout this chapter were made during interviews with Kurt Wootton, July 2011.

4. Cushman, *Fires in the Mind.*

5. Graham and Perin, *Writing Next,* 15.

6. Berger, *Ethic of Excellence,* 103.

7. Ibid., 99.

8. Stevenson and Deasy, *Third Space,* 18.

9. Greene, *Releasing the Imagination.*

10. Wilhelm, *"You Gotta BE the Book."*

11. Seuss, *The Lorax.*

12. Ibid.

13. The term *layering* used in this context was coined by Cynthia Weiss, Arnold Aprill, Robert Possehl, and Kurt Wootton at a teacher institute led by Chicago Arts Partnerships in Education, June 2009.

14. Phillips, *Ernest Hemingway on Writing,* 134

15. Krashen and Terrell, *Natural Approach.*

Chapter 7

1. *New York Times,* February 24, 2010.

2. Santiago Medina is a pseudonym.

3. Comments made by Richard Kinslow throughout this chapter were made during an interview with Kurt Wootton, June 2004.

4. New London Group, *A Pedagogy of Multiliteracies*, 64.

5. Quoted in Schmoker, *Results Now*, 92.

6. Donald, "Art and Cognitive Evolution," 5.

7. Erminio Pinque, e-mail to Len Newman, January 2004.

8. Heath, "Dynamics of Completion," 134.

9. Len Newman, interview with Kurt Wootton, June 2008.

10. Horton, Freire, Bell, Gaventa, and Peters, *We Make the Road*, 27.

11. Ferreiro, "Reading and Writing," 25.

12. Delpit, *Other People's Children*, 32–33.

13. Perkins, "Foreword," v.

14. For a comprehensive discussion of exhibitions, see Sizer, *Horace's School*.

Chapter 8

1. Students' names in this chapter are pseudonyms.

2. Lerman, *Critical Response Process*.

3. *Oxford English Dictionary* online edition.

4. Clark, *Being There*.

5. Ibid., 210.

6. Ibid., 209.

7. Bransford, Brown, and Cocking, *How People Learn*; Lehrer, *How We Decide*.

8. Bransford, Brown, and Cocking, *How People Learn*.

9. Langer, *Mindfulness*; Richhart and Perkins, *Life in the Mindful Classroom*.

10. Lehrer, *How We Decide*, 250.

11. Ibid.

12. Cazden, *Classroom Discourse*, 31.

13. Langer, *Power of Mindful Learning*, 4.

14. Richhart and Perkins, *Life in the Mindful Classroom*, 29.

15. Langer cited in ibid., 29.

16. Greene, *Imagination in Teaching and Learning;* New London Group, *Pedagogy of Multiliteracies.*

Epilogue

1. Dan deCelles e-mail to Eileen Landay, December 2011.

2. Shirley Brice Heath lecture at Brown University, July 16, 2003.

3. Johnson, *Where Good Ideas Come From.*

4. Machado, *Selected Poems*, 83–85.

Works Cited

Anderson, Lorin W., and David R. Krathwohl, eds. *A Taxonomy for Learning, Teaching and Assessing.* New York: Addison, Wesley, Longman, 2001.

Anderson, Richard C. *Research Foundations for Wide Reading.* Urbana, IL: Center for the Study of Reading, 1992.

Atkins, Greg. *improv! A Handbook for the Actor.* Portsmouth, NH: Heinemann, 1994.

Atwell, Nancie. *In the Middle: New Understandings About Writing, Reading, and Learning.* 2nd ed. Portsmouth, NH: Heinemann, 1998.

———. *Lessons That Change Writers.* Portsmouth, NH: FirstHand, 2007.

———. *The Reading Zone: How to Help Kids Become Skilled, Passionate, Habitual, Critical Readers.* New York: Scholastic, 2007.

Bakhtin, Mikhail M. *The Dialogic Imagination: Four Essays.* Ed. Michael Holquist. Trans. Vadim Liaponov and Kenneth Brostrom. Austin: University of Texas Press, 1981.

Beers, Kylene, Robert Probst, and Linda Reif. *Adolescent Literacy: Turning Promise into Practice.* Portsmouth, NH: Heinemann, 2007.

Bennett, Drake. "Don't Just Stand There, Think: New Research Suggests That We Think Not Just with Our Brains but with Our Bodies." *Boston Globe*, January 13, 2008.

Berger, Ron. *An Ethic of Excellence: Building a Culture of Craftsmanship with Students.* Portsmouth, NH: Heinemann, 2003.

Berry, Wendell. "People, Land, and Community." In *The Graywolf Annual Five: Multi-Cultural Literacy.* Ed. Rick Simonson and Scott Walker. St. Paul, MN: Graywolf Press, 1988.

Boal, Augusto. *The Rainbow of Desire.* New York: Routledge, 1995.

———. *Games for Actors and Non-Actors.* 2nd ed. New York: Routledge, 2002.

Bransford, John, Ann L. Brown, and Rodney R. Cocking, eds. *How People Learn: Brain, Mind, Experience and School.* Washington, DC: National Academies Press, 1999.

Cazden, Courtney. *Classroom Discourse: The Language of Teaching and Learning.* 2nd ed. Portsmouth, NH: Heinemann, 2001.

Cisneros, Sandra. *The House on Mango Street.* New York: Vintage, 1991.

Clark, Andy. *Being There: Putting Brain, Body and World Together Again.* Cambridge, MA: MIT Press, 1998.

Clifton, Lucille. "whose side are you on?" In *Quilting Poems, 1987–1990.* Rochester, NY: BOA Editions, 2000.

Conley, David T. *College Knowledge: What It Really Takes for Students to Succeed and What We Can Do to Get Them Ready.* San Francisco: Jossey-Bass, 2008.

Cushman, Kathleen. *Fires in the Mind: What Kids Can Tell Us About Motivation and Mastery.* San Francisco: Jossey-Bass, 2010.

Davidson, Cathy N. *Now You See It: How the Brain Science of Attention Will Transform the Way We Live, Work and Learn.* New York: Viking, 2011.

Delpit, Lisa. *Other People's Children: Cultural Conflict in the Classroom.* New York: New Press, 1995.

Dickinson, Emily. "To Make a Prairie." *The Complete Poems of Emily Dickinson.* Ed. Thomas H. Johnson. Boston: Little, Brown, 1960.

Donald, Merlin. *Origins of the Modern Mind.* Cambridge, MA: Harvard University Press, 1991.

———. "Art and Cognitive Evolution." In *The Artful Mind: Cognitive Science and the Riddle of Human Creativity.* Ed. Mark Turner. New York: Oxford University Press, 2006.

Douglass, Frederick. *Narrative of the Life of Frederick Douglass: An American Slave.* New York: Barnes & Noble Classics, 2003.

Dr. Seuss [Theodor S. Geisel]. *The Lorax.* New York: Random House, 1971.

Egan, Kieran. *Imagination in Teaching and Learning: The Middle School Years.* Chicago: University of Chicago Press, 1992.

———. *The Educated Mind: How Cognitive Tools Shape Our Understanding.* Chicago: University of Chicago Press, 1997.

———. *An Imaginative Approach to Teaching.* San Francisco: John Wiley, 2005.

Ewald, Wendy. *Secret Games: Collaborative Works with Children, 1969–1999.* Zurich: Scalo Books, 2000.

Ferreiro, Emilia. "Reading and Writing in a Changing World." *Publishing Research Quarterly 16,* no. 25 (2000): 53–61.

———. *Past and Present of the Verbs to Read and to Write: Essays on Literacy.* Toronto: Groundwood Books, 2003.

Florida, Richard. *The Rise of the Creative Class and How It's Transforming Work, Leisure, Community and Everyday Life.* New York: Basic Books, 2002.

Freire, Paulo. *Education for Critical Consciousness.* New York: Continuum, 1974.

———. *Pedagogy of Hope.* New York: Continuum, 1992.

———. *Pedagogy of Freedom: Ethics, Democracy and Civic Courage.* Boston: Roman & Littlefield, 2000.

———. *Pedagogy of the Oppressed.* New York: Continuum, 2003.

Gallagher, Kelly. *Deeper Reading.* Portland, ME: Stenhouse, 2004.

Garcia Lorca, Federico. *Blood Wedding: A Play.* Trans. Ted Hughes. London: Faber & Faber, 1997.

Gardner, Howard. *Frames of Mind: The Theory of Multiple Intelligences.* New York: Basic Books, 1993.

———. *The Unschooled Mind: How Children Think and How Schools Should Teach.* New York: Basic Books, 1993.

———. *Multiple Intelligences: New Horizons in Theory and Practice.* New York: Basic Books, 2006.

Gee, James P. "What Is Literacy?" In *Rewriting Literacy: Culture and the Discourse of the Other.* Ed. Candace Mitchell and Kathleen Weiler. New York: Bergin & Garvey, 1992.

———. *Social Linguistics and Literacies: Ideology in Discourses.* Bristol, PA: Taylor & Francis, 1996.

Goldin-Meadow, Susan. *Hearing Gesture: How Our Hands Help Us Think.* Cambridge, MA: Belknap Press, 2005.

Gonzalez, Norma, Luis Moll, and Cathy Amanti, eds. *Funds of Knowledge: Theorizing Practices in Households, Communities and Classrooms.* Hillsdale, NJ: Erlbaum, 2005.

Goodlad, John. *A Place Called School.* 2nd ed. New York: McGraw Hill, 2004.

Graham, Steve, and Dolores Perin. *Writing Next: Effective Strategies to Improve Writing of Adolescents in Middle and High Schools.* Washington, DC: Alliance for Excellent Education, 2007.

Graves, Donald. *A Fresh Look at Writing.* Portsmouth, NH: Heinemann, 1994.

Greene, Maxine. *Releasing the Imagination: Essays on Education, the Arts, and Social Change.* San Francisco: Jossey-Bass, 1998.

Greenfield, Patricia. "Technology and Informal Education: What Is Taught, What Is Learned." *Science* 323, no. 2 (2009): 69–71.

Harvey, Stephanie, and Anne Goudvis. *Strategies That Work: Teaching Comprehension for Understanding and Engagement.* 2nd ed. Portland, ME: Stenhouse, 2007.

Heath, Shirley Brice. "Seeing Our Way into Learning." *Cambridge Journal of Education* 30, no. 1 (2000): 121–132.

———. "Dynamics of Completion." In *The Artful Mind: Cognitive Science and the Riddle of Human Creativity*. Ed. Mark Turner. New York: Oxford University Press, 2006.

———. *Ways with Words: Language, Life and Work in Communities and Classrooms*. 2nd ed. New York: Cambridge University Press, 2006.

Heath, Shirley Brice, with Adelma Roach. "Imaginative Actuality: Learning in the Arts During the Nonschool Hours." In *Champions of Change: The Impact of the Arts on Learning*. Ed. Edward B. Fiske. Washington, DC: Arts Education Partnership, 1999.

Heathcote, Dorothy, and Gavin Bolton. *Drama for Learning: Dorothy Heathcote's "Mantle of the Expert" Approach to Education*. Portsmouth, NH: Heinemann, 1995.

Hetland, Lois, Ellen Winner, Shirley Veenema, and Kimberly N. Sheridan. *Studio Thinking: The Real Benefits of Visual Arts Education*. New York: Teachers College Press, 2007.

Hispanics: A People in Motion. Washington, DC: Pew Hispanic Center, 2005.

Horton, Myles, Paulo Freire, Brenda Bell, John Gaventa, and John Peters. *We Make the Road by Walking: Conversations on Education and Social Change*. Philadelphia: Temple University Press, 1990.

Johnson, Steven. *Where Good Ideas Come From: The Natural History of Innovation*. New York: Penguin, 2010.

Keene, Ellen, and Susan Zimmerman. *Mosaic of Thought*. 2nd ed. Portsmouth, NH: Heinemann, 2008.

King, Nancy. *Storymaking and Drama: An Approach to Teaching Language and Literature at the Secondary and Postsecondary Levels*. Portsmouth, NH: Heinemann, 1993.

Koch, Kenneth. *Wishes, Lies and Dreams: Teaching Children to Write Poetry*. New York: HarperCollins, 1970.

Krashen, Stephen, and Tracy D. Terrell. *The Natural Approach: Language Acquisition in the Classroom*. Hayward, CA: Alemany Press, 1983.

Kress, Gunther. *Literacy in the New Media Age*. New York: Routledge, 2003.

Landay, Eileen. "Performance as the Foundation for a Secondary School Literacy Program: A Bakhtinian Perspective." In *Bakhtinian Perspectives on Language, Literacy and Learning*. Ed. Arnetha F. Ball and Sarah Warshauer Freedman. New York: Cambridge University Press, 2004.

————. "Give Me Moor Proof: *Othello* in Seventh Grade." *English Journal 95*, no. 1 (2005): 39–46.

Langer, Ellen J. *Mindfulness.* Reading, MA: Addison-Wesley, 1989.

————. *The Power of Mindful Learning.* Reading, MA: Perseus Books, 1997.

Lave, Jean, and Etienne Wenger. *Situated Learning: Legitimate Peripheral Participation.* New York: Cambridge University Press, 1991.

Lee, Carol D., and Peter Smagorinsky, eds. *Vygotskian Perspectives on Literacy Research: Constructing Meaning Through Collaborative Inquiry.* New York: Cambridge University Press, 2000.

Lee, Harper. *To Kill a Mockingbird.* New York: HarperCollins, 1960.

Lehrer, Jonah. *How We Decide.* New York: Houghton Mifflin Harcourt, 2009.

Lerman, Liz, and John Borstel. *Liz Lerman's Critical Response Process: A Method for Getting Useful Feedback on Anything You Make, from Dance to Dessert.* Washington, DC: Liz Lerman Dance Exchange, 2003.

Lopez, Barry. *Crossing Open Ground.* New York: Random House, 1989.

Machado, Antonio. *Antonio Machado: Selected Poems.* Trans. Betty Jean Craige. Louisiana State University Press, 1978.

Macrorie, Ken. *The I-Search Paper.* Portsmouth, NH: Boynton Cook, 1988.

Mandell, Jan, and Jennifer Wolf. *Acting, Learning and Change: Creating Original Plays with Adolescents.* Portsmouth, NH: Heinemann, 2003.

Martin, Nancy. *Mostly About Writing: Selected Essays.* Portsmouth, NH: Heinemann, 1983.

Mehan, Hugh. *Learning Lessons: Social Organization in the Classroom.* Cambridge, MA: Harvard University Press, 1979.

Meier, Deborah. *In Schools We Trust: Creating Communities of Learning in an Era of Testing and Standardization.* Boston: Beacon Press, 2003.

Moll, Luis C., and James B. Greenberg. "Creating Zones of Possibilities: Combining Social Contexts for Instruction." In *Vygotsky and Education.* Ed. Luis C. Moll. New York: Cambridge University Press, 1990.

Nagy, William E., and Richard C. Anderson. "How Many Words Are There in Printed English?" *Reading Research Quarterly* 19, no. 3 (1984): 304–330.

New London Group. "A Pedagogy of Multiliteracies: Designing Social Futures." *Harvard Educational Review 66*, no. 1 (1996): 60–92.

Nieto, Sonia. *The Light in Their Eyes: Creating Multicultural Learning Communities.* New York: Teachers College Press, 1999.

Obama, Barack. *Dreams from My Father: A Story of Race and Inheritance.* New York: Crown, 2007.

————. "A More Perfect Union." National Constitution Center, Philadelphia, PA, March 18, 2008.

Ornstein, Allan C., and Daniel U. Levine. *Foundations of Education*. Boston: Houghton Mifflin, 2006.

Ovid. *Metamorphoses*. Trans. Rolfe Humphries. Bloomington: Indiana University Press, 1960.

Pennac, Daniel. *The Rights of the Reader*. Cambridge, MA: Candlewick Press, 2008.

Perkins, David. *Smart Schools: From Training Memories to Educating Minds*. New York: Free Press, 1992.

————. "Foreword." In *Studio Thinking: The Real Benefits of Visual Arts Education*. By Lois Hetland, Ellen Winner, Shirley Veenema, and Kimberly N. Sheridan. New York: Teachers College Press, 2007.

Phillips, Larry W., ed. *Ernest Hemingway on Writing*. New York: Scribner's, 1999.

Pink, Daniel. *A Whole New Mind: Why Right-Brainers Will Rule the Future*. New York: Penguin, 2005.

Plutarch. "On Listening to Lectures." Trans. F. C. Babbitt. In *Moralia*. Vol. 1. Cambridge, MA: Harvard University Press, 1927.

Podlozny, Ann. "Strengthening Verbal Skills Through the Use of Classroom Drama: A Clear Link." *Journal of Aesthetic Education* 34, no. 3 (2000): 239–275.

Rabkin, Nick. "Learning in the Arts." In *Putting the Arts in the Picture: Reframing Education in the 21st Century*. Ed. Nick Rabkin and Robin Redmont. Chicago: Columbia College Chicago, 2004.

Ravitch, Diane. *The Death and Life of the Great American School System: How Testing and Choice Are Undermining Education*. New York: Basic Books, 2010.

Reddy, Michael J. "The Conduit Metaphor: A Case of Frame Conflict in Our Language about Language." In *Metaphor and Thought*. Ed. Andrew Ortony. New York: Cambridge University Press, 1979.

Ritchhart, Ron, and David Perkins. "Life in the Mindful Classroom: Nurturing the Disposition of Mindfulness." *Journal of Social Issues* 56, no. 1 (2000): 27–47.

Robinson, Randal F. *Unlocking Shakespeare's Language*. Urbana, IL: National Council of Teachers of English, 1988.

Rohd, Michael. *Theater for Community, Conflict, and Dialogue: The Hope Is Vital Training Manual*. Portsmouth, NH: Heinemann, 1998.

Rosenblatt, Louise. *Literature as Exploration*. New York: Modern Language Association, 1965.

————. *The Reader, the Text and the Poem: The Transactional Theory of the Literary Work*. Carbondale: Southern Illinois University Press, 1978.

Rumi, Jalal. *The Essential Rumi: Expanded Edition.* Trans. Coleman Barks. New York: HarperOne, 2004.

Said, Edward. *Humanism and Democratic Criticism.* New York: Columbia University Press, 2004.

Schmoker, Mike. *Results Now: How We Can Achieve Unprecedented Improvements in Teaching and Learning.* Alexandria, VA: Association for Supervision and Curriculum Development, 2006.

Schön, Donald. *The Reflective Practitioner: How Professionals Think in Action.* New York: Basic Books, 1983.

Seligman, Martin E. P. *Helplessness.* New York: Freeman, 1992.

Sizer, Theodore R. *Horace's School: Redesigning the American High School.* New York: Mariner Books, 1997.

———. *The Red Pencil: Convictions from Experiences in Education.* New Haven, CT: Yale University Press, 2004.

Slater, Candace. *Stories on a String: The Brazilian Literatura de Cordel.* Berkeley: University of California Press, 1982.

Smith, Frank. *Joining the Literacy Club: Further Essays into Education.* Portsmouth, NH: Heinemann, 1998.

Smyth, Laura, and Lauren Stevenson, eds. *You Want to Be Part of Everything: The Arts, Community and Learning.* Washington, DC: Arts Education Partnership, 2003.

Snow, Catherine E., Michelle V. Porche, Patton O. Tabors, and Stephanie R. Harris. *Is Literacy Enough? Pathways to Academic Success for Adolescents.* Baltimore: Paul H. Brookes, 2007.

Spolin, Viola. *Improvisation for the Theater.* Evanston, IL: Northwestern University Press, 1963.

Stanovich, Keith E. "Matthew Effects in Reading: Some Consequences of Individual Differences in the Acquisition of Literacy." *Reading Research Quarterly* 21, no. 4 (1986): 360–407.

Steinbeck, John. *The Pearl.* New York: Bantam Books, 1975.

Stevenson, Lauren, and Richard Deasy. *Third Space: When Learning Matters.* Washington, DC: Arts Education Partnership, 2005.

Tan, Amy. *Joy Luck Club.* New York: Penguin, 2006.

Thompson, Mary Jo, and Becca Barniskis. *The Artful Teaching and Learning Handbook.* Minneapolis: Perpich Center for Arts Education, 2005.

Thoreau, Henry D. *Walden and Other Writings of Henry David Thoreau.* Ed. Brooks Atkinson. New York: Random House, 1950.

To Read or Not to Read: A Matter of National Consequence. Research Report No. 47. Washington, DC: NEA, 2007.

UN Population Commission. *Report: Third Session.* UN Doc. E/805. Lake Success, New York: United Nations, 1948.

Wagner, Betty Jane. *Educational Drama and Language Arts: What the Research Shows.* Portsmouth, NH: Heinemann, 1998.

Wenger, Etienne. *Communities of Practice: Learning, Meaning and Identity.* New York: Cambridge University Press, 1998.

Whitman, Walt. *Complete Poetry and Collected Prose.* Library of America, 1982.

Wiggins, Grant. "What Is an Essential Question?" http://www.authenticeducation. org/ae_bigideas/article.lasso?artid=53.

Wiggins, Grant, and Jay McTighe. *Understanding by Design.* 2nd ed. Upper Saddle River, NJ: Prentice Hall, 2005.

Wilhelm, Jeffrey. *"You Gotta BE the Book": Teaching Engaged and Reflective Reading with Adolescents.* New York: Teachers College Press, 1997.

Wilson, August. *The Piano Lesson.* New York: Plume, 1990.

Wiske, Martha Stone, ed. *Teaching for Understanding: Linking Research with Practice.* San Francisco: Jossey-Bass, 1998.

Wolf, Shelby, Brian Edmiston, and Patricia Enciso. "Drama Worlds: Places of the Heart, Head, Voice and Hand in Dramatic Interpretation." In *Handbook of Research on Teaching Literacy Through the Communicative and Visual Arts.* Ed. James Flood, Shirley Brice Heath, and Diane Lapp. New York: Macmillan, 1997.

Wootton, Kurt. "Community This and Community That." In *You Want to Be Part of Everything: The Arts, Community, and Learning.* Ed. Laura Smyth and Lauren Stevenson. Washington, DC: Arts Education Partnership, 2005.

Zaporah, Ruth. *Action Theater: The Improvisation of Presence.* Berkeley, CA: North Atlantic Books, 1995.

Acknowledgments

IT IS CUSTOMARY to thank the authors' families at the conclusion of an acknowledgments section. We would like to reverse that custom and offer a place of honor to our families by thanking them at the outset.

Kurt would like to thank his parents, Jim and Alice Wootton. Through their own work as public school educators, they demonstrated how one can teach creatively and critically. He would also like to thank his wife, María del Mar Patrón Vázquez, for inspiring and encouraging him to take on new challenges, whether it be establishing an organization in another country or learning to live in a new language. He is especially grateful to his beautiful daughter, Sandra, for bringing so much *alegria* into his life.

Eileen watches with pride and wonder as children and grandchildren grow and contribute in wonderful ways to a world full of surprise and change. Who ever would have imagined? First the typewriter, then the word processor, now a veritable multitude of mediums and devices to record and convey words and images—in your hands to build a better, more equitable world. Her appreciation and deepest affection to Roger, Steven, Max, Murray and Alan Rosenbaum, and Pam Yoder. And to Sandy Chabot and Jerry Landay, companions and friends.

We want to thank our friend and colleague Nancy Hoffman for helping to launch and create a solid foundation for the ArtsLiteracy Project. This book and the project it describes have roots that are both wide and deep. Established in classrooms in Indiana and Maine, the work gained shape and strength in Rhode Island—principally in the Education Department at Brown University and in Providence area schools. Now, thanks to colleagues and students, it continues to grow in its home territory and more broadly in Maine, California, New York, Minnesota, Mexico, Brazil, the Dominican Republic, and beyond.

The Bread Loaf School of English has always been a magical place, never more than those years when the esteemed Dixie Goswami brought together a group of thinkers, writers, teachers—including Nancie Atwell, Jimmy Britton, Peter Elbow, Donald Graves, Shirley Heath, Ken Macrorie, Nancy Martin, and Jim Moffett—to challenge and change the way reading and writing are taught in American schools and to provide a foundation for linking literacy and the arts. Appreciation to Jim and Lucy Maddox for their leadership and encouragement. Special thanks to the invaluable Courtney Cazden, who has been a consistent, ever-present source of advice and support, beginning that day on the porch at the Inn.

Our work would not be what it is without the opportunity to learn from many talented and dedicated teachers and artists. We would especially like to thank Patricia Sobral, Mary Beth Meehan, João Kulcsar, Frankslayne Paranista, Flavio Ricardo Borges, Magdalena Gómez, Ben Johnson, Fred Sullivan, Angela Brazil, Mauro Hantman, Phyllis Kay, Rachael Hantman, Michael Paul, Raidge, Abigail Jefferson, @Peace, Melody Thompson, Rick Benjamin, Deanna Camputaro, Deloris Grant, Jonathan Goodman, Anna Kuperman, Shivohn Garcia, Maia Olff, Nicole Smith, Kate Hewitt, and Laura Maxwell and to remember with affection ArtsLiteracy teachers Dave Claflin and Nancy Carnevale.

Thanks especially to Len Newman, Daniel Soares, Richard Kinslow, Bobby Marchand, Robin Yates, Theresa Toomey Fox, Dan DeCelles, Erminio Pinque, Karla Hernando, Jessica Robertson, Kevin Gibbs, and Cynthia Weiss for opening their classrooms and spending time with us talking about their work as educators and artists.

Many Brown University students worked with us over the years helping with documentation and research, recording teaching practices, teaching in classrooms, and providing support for the daily life of the project. We would especially like to thank Maggie Blake, Michael Gregory, Sarah Leibel,

Jessica Delforge, Rosa Miller, Megan Sandberg-Zakian, Ellie Davis, Sarah Kwon, Reif Larson, Gina Coggio and Erica Saleh for their dedication to the project during and beyond their time as students at Brown. We recognize also the contributions of the many Brown MAT/UTEP students and the students in ED 169, "Literacy, Community and the Arts," who have learned alongside us and put the work to use.

Friends and teachers who have been important to our personal and teaching lives outside of the project are Andy Lindauer, Shirley Everett, John Hanlon, Deb Christenson, Robert Allwarden, Daniel Bisaccio, Elizabeth Bailey, Liz Hollander, Carla and John Rensenbrink, Anne Wescott Dodd, and Tom and Sarah Gleason.

Our deepest gratitude to the always innovative and forward-thinking ArtsLiteracy staff: Angela Richardson, Jori Ketten, Nancy Safian, John Holdridge, Nadia Mahdi, Elizabeth Keiser, Steve Kidd, Michael Baron, and Suzy Box. Without them, none of the work described in this book would have been possible.

Many colleagues in the Education Department helped to give the project a home at Brown, including Larry Wakeford, Bil Johnson, Cynthia Garcia Coll, Carl Kaestle, Warren Simmons, Adie Becker, Dennie Palmer Wolf, Carin Algava, Ann D'Abrosca, Karl Dominey, Polly Ulichny, Chris Amirault, John Modell, and Laura Snyder.

Our thanks to the educational leaders, organizational directors, and researchers who have collaborated with us and supported the development of ArtsLiteracy in different venues. They include Donald King, Sherilyn Brown, Ewa Pytowska, Maureen Chevrette, Lauren Stevenson, Doris Sommer, Steve Seidel, Becky Coustan, Eileen Mackin, Bob Mackin, Oskar Eustis, Ann Galligan, Rob Horowitz, Nick Donohue, Karen Romer, Carolyn Sheehan, and Kyleen Carpenter.

Recently, colleagues at Habla have helped to move ArtsLiteracy work forward. They include Arnold Aprill, Nick Rabkin, Jim McLaughlin, Sam Seidel, Charly Barbera, Laura Riebock, Nidia Schuhmacher, and William Estrada.

The brilliant Jan Mandell and her colleagues in St. Paul, Minnesota, have become full partners in ArtsLiteracy work, applying it consistently and in innovative ways across the school district and beyond. Our thanks to Darlene Fry, Kimberly Colbert, Anthony Jacobs, Clara Hutchinson, Matt Shipman, Kat Jordahl, Kaye Peters, Eliza Rasheed, Cornelius Rish, Micheal Thompson, James "Jayydubb" Williams, T. Mychael Rambo, Mary Mackbee, and Naomi Larson. Our thanks, too, to the phenomenal student members—past and present—of the Central Touring Theater and the ArtsLiteracy Leadership Team. And in Minneapolis, thanks to Mary Jo Thompson, Dudley Voight, and Crystal Spring.

We are deeply grateful to Jim Wootton and Brown student Rebekah Bergman for taking the time to read and edit multiple drafts of our book. Thanks to our colleagues and friends Kathleen Cushman, Gail Burnaford, and Richard Deasy for reviewing the manuscript at various stages and offering their indispensable guidance. Douglas Clayton at the Harvard Education Publishing Group was enthusiastic and encouraging through the entire process. We thank him for his constant support in helping to bring our book to life. We'd also like to thank Sumita Mukherji, Laura Madden, and Joanna Craig for spending hours preparing the manuscript and getting the word out about *A Reason to Read*.

We've always suspected that the visionary Shirley Brice Heath is more than one person, so prolific is she. A long and precious friendship has taught us that, yes, one person can do it all.

This book was written with the support of the Ford Foundation. We would especially like to thank Cyrus Driver for recognizing the value of the ArtsLiteracy Project's work. Initial funding for the project was also provided by the Spencer Foundation, the Rhode Island Foundation, the U.S. Department of Education, the National Endowment for the Arts, the Education Foundation of America, and the Providence Journal Charitable Foundation.

About the Authors

Eileen Landay was the Clinical Professor of English Education at Brown University, director of Brown's MAT Program in English Education, and faculty director of Brown Summer High School from 1993 to 2006. She is the cofounder and codirector of the ArtsLiteracy Project, which in 2005 received the President's Commission on the Arts and Humanities "Coming Up Taller" Award. She holds an appointment as adjunct senior lecturer at Brown, where she continues to teach. She also teaches and consults regionally and nationally on adolescent literacy development, arts integration, and English education.

Before coming to Brown, Landay was a teacher of secondary and elementary English, the English Language Arts consultant for the Maine Department of Education, chief reader for the Maine Educational Assessment, and a poet in the state's schools, funded through the Maine Arts Commission. She edited *Maine Speaks: An Anthology of Maine Literature* (Maine Writers & Pubs Alliance, 1996) and is the author of children's fiction, several books on teaching poetry, and numerous articles and book chapters, including the articles "Across the Doorsill: Extending Learning with Students in Mind and Body," in *Voices in Urban Education* (2007) and "Narrative Interviews: An Approach to Studying Teaching and Learning in English Classrooms," in *High School Journal* (February/March 2001). She holds an MA from the Bread Loaf School of English at Middlebury College and an EdD from Harvard Graduate School of Education.

Kurt Wootton is the cofounder and codirector of the ArtsLiteracy Project in the Education Department at Brown University. His work in urban schools with diverse populations has led him to work in different countries in Latin America, particularly Brazil and Mexico. He is also the codirector of Habla: The Center for Language and Culture in Mérida, Mexico, a combination language school, education center, and community-based arts organization. With a specialty in creative literacy pedagogies, teacher professional development, and organizational change, Wootton works with teachers and administrators to help design schools and organizations that are creative, meaningful, and welcoming places.

Previously he worked as an urban school reform consultant for the Providence School District and has led literacy initiatives for the Boston Public Schools, the St. Paul Public Schools, the Central Falls School District, and Plan Estratégico de Mérida, Mexico. Wootton has been called on to offer keynote speeches and workshops in a variety of settings, including Harvard University, Middlebury College, SmART Schools, Chicago Arts Partnerships in Education, Florida Atlantic University, the University of Maryland, Senac University in Sao Paulo, the Arts Education Partnership, as well as at numerous conferences.

He writes about education on his own blog, *The Education Labyrinth*, as well as for the *Huffington Post*. His publications include "Thinking Differently: The Arts and School Reform," *College Board* (2010); "A Constant Search: Arts-Integration in Cross-Cultural Environments," *Teaching Artist Journal* (July 2008); and, with Eileen Landay, Mary Beth Meehan, A. Leonard Newman, and Donald W. King, "Postcards from America: Linking Classrooms and Community in an ESL class," *English Journal* (2005). He divides his time between Mexico and the United States.

Index